AMERICAN NATURE GUIDES

SHOREBIRDS OF NORTH AMERICA

AMERICAN NATURE GUIDES

SHOREBIRDS OF NORTH AMERICA

ALAN RICHARDS

GALLERY BOOKS
An Imprint of W. H. Smith Publishers Inc.
112 Madison Avenue
New York City 10016

This edition first published in 1991 by Gallery Books,
an imprint of W H Smith Publishers, Inc,
112 Madison Avenue, New York 10016

Published in England by Dragon's World Ltd,
Limpsfield and London

Designer: David Allen
Editor: Trish Burgess
Editorial Director: Pippa Rubinstein

ISBN 0 8317 6962 9

Printed in Singapore

Key to maps
Yellow areas indicate breeding ranges
Blue areas indicate winter ranges
Green areas indicate where breeding and winter ranges overlap

Contents

Introduction

Among the world's approximately 8500 species of birds, there are some 202 that are generally called "shorebirds" by American birdwatchers ("waders" by Europeans). Most of these birds are placed in two families, namely the Sandpipers (Scolopacidae), 85 species, and the Plovers (Charadriidae), 62 species. Additionally, the Oystercatchers (Haematopodidae) six species, Avocets and Stilts (Recurvirostridae), six species, and Stone Curlews (Burhinidae), nine species, are also readily recognized as belonging within this group. However, the terminology also includes the Lilytrotters

(Jacanidae), seven species, Painted Snipe (Rostratulidae), two species, Coursers and Pratincoles (Glareolidae), 17 species, the Crab Plover (Dromididae), one species, the Ibisbill (Ibidorhynchidae), one species, Seed Snipes (Thincoridae), four species and the Sheathbills (Chionidae), two species.

The majority of these latter mentioned families are not ostensibly shorebirds, nor do they spend much of their lives wading; nevertheless, all these 12 families belong to the sub-order Charadrii of the order Charadriiformes (which additionally embraces the gulls, the terns and the auks). This book, however, does not set out to cover all the Charadrii worldwide, but concentrates only on

Hilbre Island, Dee Estuary

those species in the first five families mentioned above that breed in Northern America (Neararctic). In all, 45 species are dealt with in detail. Europe and North America share many of the same species of shorebirds, either as breeding species or as visitors, and these vagrant species are also dealt with in this book.

Shorebirds are undoubtedly some of the most interesting of the world's birds and also some of the greatest avian travelers, their migrations spanning the globe. In addition, they have great diversity of plumage, many showing complete changes of appearance from summer to winter. Their manner of feeding varies enormously, while their displays and courtship involve some of the

Mixed flock of waders at Hilbre Island including Sanderling, Dunlin and Turnstone

most amazing demonstrations of flight and vocalization to be found within any bird group.

Though we call these birds shorebirds, it is only for part of their lives that they actually live up to this term. In the breeding season many species nest miles from the sea, some on barren tundras, others in muskeg swamps, others on prairie lands and a few in arid situations. If any generality of existence can be ascribed to them for all times of the year, it is as birds of open spaces (except perhaps for the American Woodcock). It is certainly during the winter months that they more noticeably live up to their name of shorebirds, for this is when they are mainly to be found on the coast, haunting mudflats, estuaries, and marshes, where they often form huge concentrations, their daily routine dictated by the rise

and fall of the tides. It is in such a setting that most observers are familiar with these birds, and we probably know more about their lives for this part of the year. Even today, we have scant knowledge of the breeding biology of a number of species, and only in recent times have the nests of some actually been discovered.

In recent years, growing concern for the environment and its wildlife has led to a greater interest and study of shorebirds, particularly as much of the wetland habitat they use has been lost to development, and many other areas are under threat.

In North America concern and interest in shorebirds has never been more evident. It is only in relatively recent times that many of these birds have begun to come back in anything like their former numbers, largely thanks to the introduction of hunting restrictions

Waders on a Florida beach

Golden Plovers

and the setting up of many wildlife reserves throughout North America where they can exist in safety and be viewed by the growing army of birders.

Alan Richards

Breeding Species or Regular Migrants

American Black Oystercatcher

Haematopus bachmani 17–18in

Nest A simple shallow scrape on rocks
Egg clutch 1–3, but usually 2
Egg color Stone background blotched with black
Laid April–May
Incubation 24–29 days
Fledging 40 days

Identification A large, heavily-built shorebird with all-black plumage, having a brown tinge to the back, wings and tail. This renders them quite difficult to pick out against dark rocks. However, adults have an orange-red bill, a yellow eye with red eye-ring and dull gray-flesh legs, which quickly identify the species. Both sexes are similar. Young birds have duller legs, and a bill with a darker tip. Juveniles also have fine brown fringes to the feathers of their upperparts.

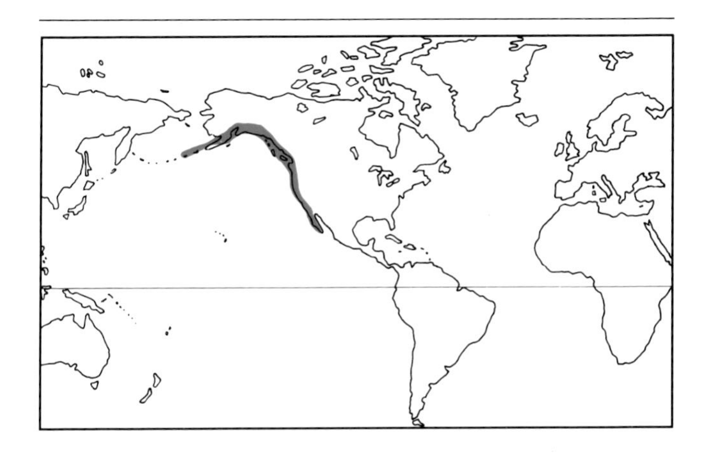

Voice Similar to other Oystercatchers, including a shrill piping "peep-peep-peep" and "pee-up" note.
Habitat Prefers rockier coastlines to American Oystercatcher, feeding singly with small groups on rocky reefs and islets; also at times to be found on adjacent beaches.
Food Similar to other species of Oystercatcher and feeds in the same way.
Range Found along the Pacific coast from the Aleutians south to Baja, California.
Movements Basically sedentary, but a little more widespread in the fall and winter. Never away from the coast.

RECORD OF SIGHTINGS	
Date ______	Date ______
Place ______	Place ______
Male(s) ______ Female(s) ______	Male(s) ______ Female(s) ______
Immature ______ Eclipse ______	Immature ______ Eclipse ______
Behavior Notes	

American Oystercatcher

Haematopus palliatus 16–18in

Nest Scrape in shingle or sand
Egg clutch 2 or 3
Egg color Stone background blotched with black
Laid Usually April–May
Incubation 28 days
Fledging 28 days

Identification When viewed at a distance, it appears to be a basically black and white bird with a long red bill. At close quarters it can be seen that the back and wing coverts are, in fact, brown. Additionally, the yellow eye, red eye-ring and pale flesh-colored legs make it one of the more easily identifiable shorebirds, especially in flight, when the conspicuous white wing bar, white rump and dark tail further enhance the typical pied look of this species. Both sexes are similar in appearance.
Voice The usual alarm call is a characteristic "kleep, kleep, kleep." Small groups frequently perform piping displays which are a development of the "kleep" note, ending in a long "kleepering" trill.

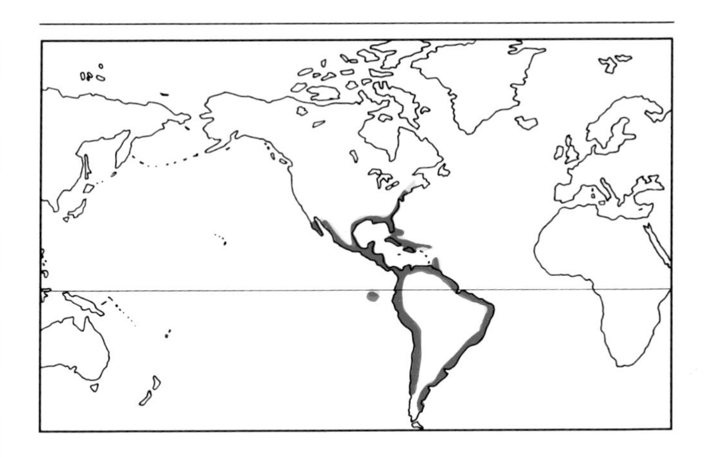

Habitat Prefers large expanses of relatively undisturbed sand and mudflats. Nests on shingle and dunes.
Food Molluscs form a major part of its diet, particularly coon oysters, cockles and mussels, which it prises open with its chisel-like bill.
Range Mainly found along the Atlantic coastal strip from Long Island south to New Jersey. Currently expanding northwards, recolonizing areas from which it has been driven by excessive shooting; formerly occurred as far north as Labrador. On the western seaboard, distribution fairly static where found sparingly along the Californian coast.
Movement Mainly sedentary, never moving any great distance from the sea.

RECORD OF SIGHTINGS	
Date ______	Date ______
Place ______	Place ______
Male(s) ______ Female(s) ______	Male(s) ______ Female(s) ______
Immature ______ Eclipse ______	Immature ______ Eclipse ______
Behavior Notes	

American Avocet

Recurvirostra americana 17–19in

Nest A shallow depression scraped out by female
Egg clutch 4
Egg color Pale ashy-yellow to green-brown, evenly spotted with dark brown
Laid April-June
Incubation 24 days
Fledging Up to 35 days

Identification During the breeding season, this large, shy, unconfiding bird has a bright brownish-orange head and neck, replacing the dull gray and white of winter plumage, and contrasting markedly with the black and white striped upperparts. With its needle-thin upturned bill (more so in the female), long blue-gray legs and white upperparts, this species is almost impossible to misidentify. In flight the shape is most distinctive, with neck and legs fully extended. The fast, direct wing-beats give an almost dart-like appearance as it dashes low over land or sea.
Voice On its breeding territory particularly, utters an incessant and penetrating "pleet" note.
Habitat Breeds around saline and alkaline lakes and pools. Outside breeding seasons all types of water habitat may be utilized.

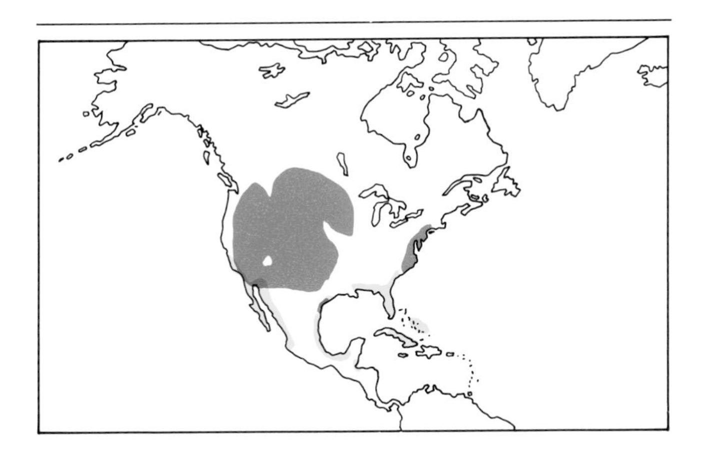

Food A variety of foodstuffs are obtained by sieving or scooping with a sweeping motion of the bill, including dragonfly nymphs, water boatmen, beetles, insects and their larvae. Seeds are also taken, as available.

Range Stretches from west coast to central USA, and to west central parts of southern Canada, including the states of Saskatchewan, Minnesota, Utah and Colorado. There are also sporadic occurrences in Texas, New Mexico, and the west coast of California.

Movements Migrates to southern parts of breeding range, and adjacent coasts of north central America. Occasionally recorded north to New Brunswick and southward to the Caribbean.

RECORD OF SIGHTINGS	
Date ______	Date ______
Place ______	Place ______
Male(s) ______ Female(s) ______	Male(s) ______ Female(s) ______
Immature ______ Eclipse ______	Immature ______ Eclipse ______
Behavior Notes	

Black-winged Stilt

Himantopus himantopus 14–16in

Nest Can be shallow scrape on dry land, or a substantial structure in shallow water
Egg clutch 4
Egg color Stone-colored, evenly spotted and blotched with dark brown
Laid May
Incubation 23 days
Fledging 28 days

Identification A slender bird, readily identified by its extremely long pink legs, needle-like black bill and simple black and white color. Most of its length is accounted for by legs and bill. The body is approximately the same size as most *Tringa* waders but has a somewhat diminutive head, in addition to a long slim neck. Both male and female have quite extensive areas of black on the head.
Voice Noisy, excitable birds, they have a high pitched "kik, kik,kik" alarm call. Also has a single "kek" note uttered as a contact call.

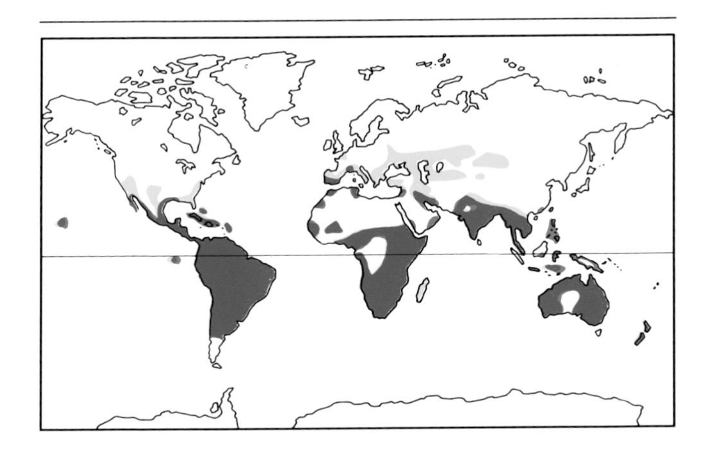

Habitat Both fresh and salt-water marshes, lagoons, saltpans, sewage farms, inland lakes.
Food Strides through shallow water seeking out all larval forms of insects, molluscs, worms and small fish.
Range Found in all continents, except Antarctica.
Movements Migratory in the northern part of its range, leaving Eurasia and northern parts of USA in the fall for tropical quarters. Returns to nesting areas, often migrating in pairs or social groups.

RECORD OF SIGHTINGS	
Date ______ Place ______ Male(s) ____ Female(s) ____ Immature ____ Eclipse ____	Date ______ Place ______ Male(s) ____ Female(s) ____ Immature ____ Eclipse ____
Behavior Notes	

Snowy Plover

Charadrius alexandrinus 6–7in

Nest Scrape in dry sandy ground
Egg clutch 3
Egg color Pale buff, with a sprinkling of black spots and streaks
Laid Early May
Incubation 26 days
Fledging 28 days

Identification This small plover, smaller than a Semipalmated Plover, has long legs in proportion to its body and a characteristically prominent head and shoulders body form, with a black mark behind the eye. The upperparts are pale sandy-gray, and breeding males have a pale fawn hindcrown and sometimes all-white lores. The underparts are white, the legs gray and the bill is shortish, slender and black. There is a characteristic black shoulder patch which never forms a complete breast band. In flight the bird shows quite a slim outline with a narrow white wing bar and white sides to the tail.
Voice A soft, disyllabic "ku-whet."
Habitat Dune systems, saline coastal lagoons, inland steppe and sand desert, also large sandy rivers and lakes.

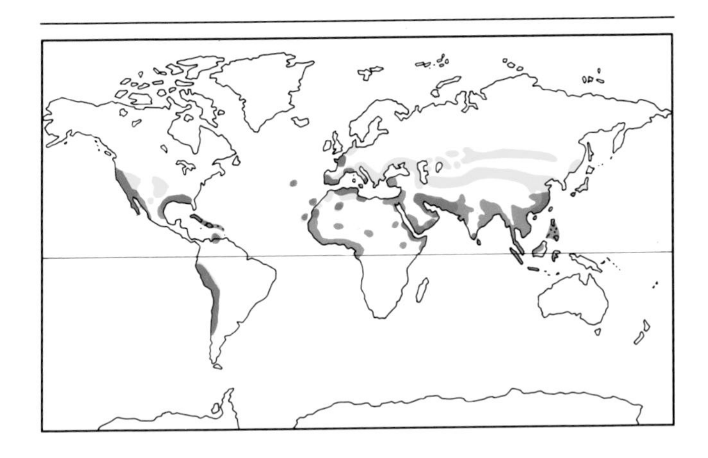

Food Small insects, molluscs, crustaceans and worms, obtained in the usual plover manner: running, stopping, pecking, in a fairly random fashion.

Range Virtually a continuous band through the warmer zones of the northern hemisphere. Fairly well represented on the west coast, in the mid-west, and around the Gulf of Mexico. Rare on east coast, except in Florida, where birds of Cuban origin spend the winter.

Movements Northern breeding birds move south to winter along the coasts of the tropics.

RECORD OF SIGHTINGS	
Date ______	Date ______
Place ______	Place ______
Male(s) ______ Female(s) ______	Male(s) ______ Female(s) ______
Immature ______ Eclipse ______	Immature ______ Eclipse ______
Behavior Notes	

Piping Plover

Charadrius melodus 6½–7½in

Nest	Scrape in dry or sandy situation
Egg clutch	4
Egg color	Light gray-brown with fine spots
Laid	May or June
Incubation	30 days
Fledging	30 days

Identification In breeding plumage this small plover has a black bar across the forehead and a black breast band which is sometimes incomplete, especially on females. The upperparts are light sandy-gray, the underparts white. The legs are orange, and so is the base of the short, black-tipped bill. All the black on the bird's forehead and breast is lost in winter, at which time the bill is also completely black, similar to the Snowy Plover, but shorter and stubbier. Juveniles are like winter adults but with slightly scaly upperparts and duller legs. In all plumages the dark eye stands out from the pale face. In flight the white wing bars and conspicuous white rump contrast with the dark gray-black flight feathers and pale gray wing coverts and body.
Voice A plaintive "peep-lo" whistle.
Habitat There are two distinct breeding areas: inland on open shorelines of shallow pools and lakes, and also among dunes and pebbly, sandy beaches along the coast. In winter it favors mudflats, coastal lagoons, and pools. At other times tidal beaches are its feeding areas.

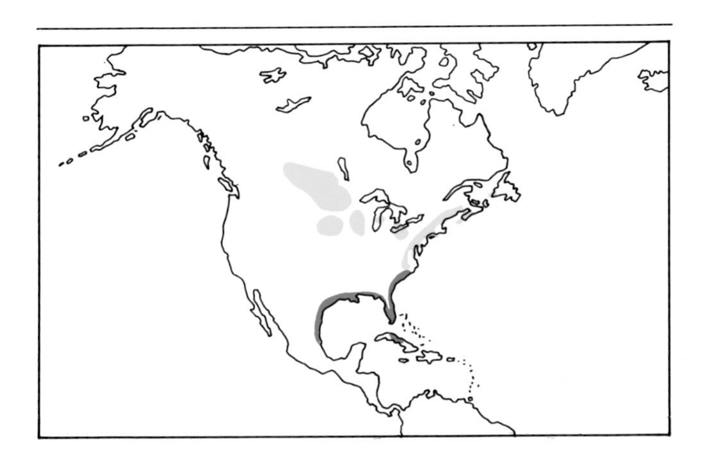

Food Worms, crustaceans, beetles, fly larvae, molluscs and insects, snatched from the surface, or by slow deliberate pecking.
Range The so-called Interior Piping Plover breeds from southern Canada, through the Dakotas to the southern shores of the Great Lakes. The Eastern Piping Plover is purely a shore-dweller, along the Atlantic coast from Newfoundland to Virginia.
Movements As the fall approaches, birds gather on the North Atlantic coast, mainly during the first part of August, and start to drift southwards for the winter. Both "Interior" and "Eastern" birds winter together along the shores of the Atlantic and the Gulf of Mexico, from South Carolina to Mexico, and the northern coast of Cuba.

RECORD OF SIGHTINGS	
Date ______________	Date ______________
Place ______________	Place ______________
Male(s) ______ Female(s) ______	Male(s) ______ Female(s) ______
Immature ____ Eclipse ______	Immature ____ Eclipse ______
Behavior Notes	

Wilson's Plover

Charadrius wilsonia 7–8in

Nest Scrape in sand or shingle
Egg clutch 3, sometimes only 2
Egg color Buff-colored, evenly spotted and blotched with brown
Laid May
Incubation 24–25 days
Fledging 21 days

Identification A small pale plover. The male in breeding plumage has a broad black neck band (which is brown in the female), while the rest of the plumage comprises dark gray-brown back and wings, distinct white collar and forehead, with the rest of the head gray, showing a thin white supercilium. Sometimes there is a cinnamon-colored ear patch. The longish, thick black bill and the pink legs are also a useful aid to identification. Juvenile birds have very scaly-looking upperparts.
Voice A weak, subdued "whit."

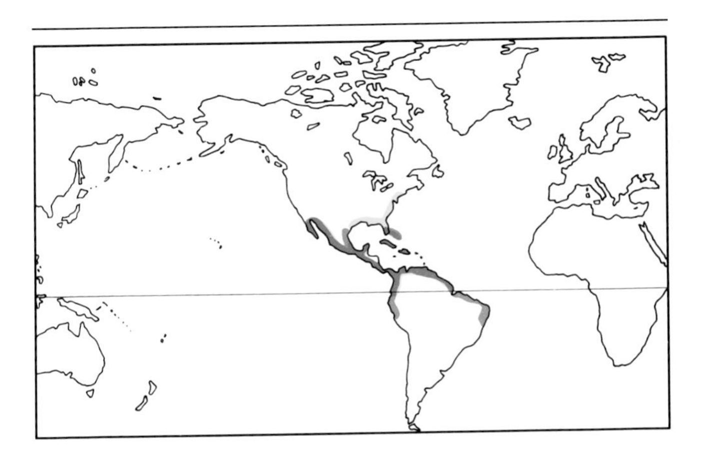

Habitat In breeding season favors shingle beaches, dunes, or dry sandy edges of coastal pools.
Food Various seashore invertebrates, particularly small crabs.
Range Most breed between the Equator and Tropic of Cancer, but in the east they are to be found nesting from Maryland almost continuously south through the West Indies to north-east Brazil. On the Pacific coast occurs from southern California through Central America to Peru.
Movements Birds largely winter within their respective breeding ranges.

RECORD OF SIGHTINGS	
Date ______	Date ______
Place ______	Place ______
Male(s) ____ Female(s) ____	Male(s) ____ Female(s) ____
Immature ____ Eclipse ____	Immature ____ Eclipse ____
Behavior Notes	

Semipalmated Plover

Charadrius semipalmatus 6½–7½in

Nest Scrape on gravelly ground
Egg clutch 3 or 4
Egg color Buff with blackish or brown speckles
Laid May–June
Incubation 24 days
Fledging 24 days

Identification A small, compact, rotund plover. Adults in breeding plumage have a white forehead, above which is a black fore-crown that meets the lower black facial line around the eye. The dark eye has a slim yellow orbital ring. Behind the eye the black ear coverts fade to light brown, which meets with the light brown of the crown and nape. There is a full white collar and below this is a full black breast band. The underparts are white. The short, stubby bill is orange with a black tip, and the legs and feet are yellowish-orange. At all ages, has a greater amount of

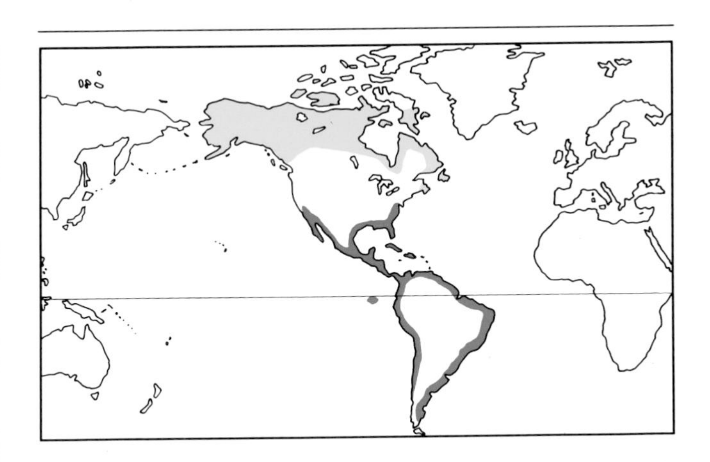

webbing between the three toes than a Ringed Plover, giving rise to the bird's common name. In flight there is a slim, yet obvious, wing bar.

Voice A sharp "chuwit."

Habitat Nests on open flat areas of tundra and gravel plains. In winter haunts wide sandy or muddy beaches and coastal lagoons.

Food Molluscs, worms and insects taken in typical plover fashion.

Range Breeding area extends from Alaska across the whole of northern Canada to Newfoundland.

Movements After nesting many move to the more southerly coasts of the USA. Others continue south to Central and South America.

RECORD OF SIGHTINGS	
Date ______	Date ______
Place ______	Place ______
Male(s) ______ Female(s) ______	Male(s) ______ Female(s) ______
Immature ______ Eclipse ______	Immature ______ Eclipse ______
Behavior Notes	

Killdeer

Charadrius vociferus 9–10in

Nest A shallow scrape on gravel or in short vegetation
Egg clutch 4
Egg color Buff-colored, with darker blotches
Laid May
Incubation 24 days
Fledging 25 days

Identification The only shorebird in North America with a double black breast band, which contrasts with the rest of its underparts, which are clean white. The head appears quite large, set on a fairly short and thick neck, showing a black and white face pattern with a brownish head crown. The upperparts are dark brown, but when the bird takes flight, a bright orange-rufous rump and upper tail is revealed. The remainder of the tail is dark brown and narrowly edged with white. Also in flight, a conspicuous white wing bar is to be seen. The legs are dull yellowish-gray, while the bright orange-red eye-ring gives the bird a deceptively gentle appearance.
Voice A loud penetrating "kill-dee" or "kill-deah," from which the bird gets its name.
Habitat Can be found from seashore up to land above 8000 feet. Favors short grassy areas and bare ground, such as meadows and

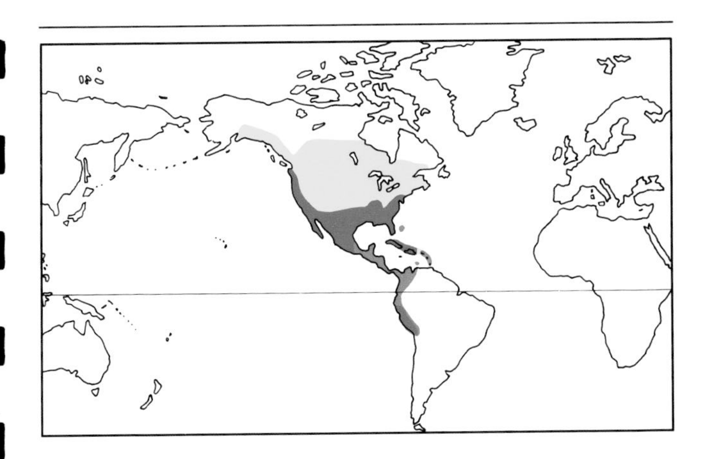

arable fields. Often found close to human habitation on gravel tracks, lawns, and golf courses.

Food Wide variety of insect food, plus worms and other invertebrates, taken in typical plover fashion. Also follows plough in search of unearthed larvae and worms.

Range Breeds widely across North America.

Movements Birds nesting in the north of its range migrate to spend the winter south of a line from California to New York. Those nesting south of that area are mainly sedentary. Killdeers are some of the first waders to be seen in northern USA and Canada in spring, with passage commencing as early as February. By May most are on their breeding ground. Return passage begins July, lasting through to November.

RECORD OF SIGHTINGS	
Date ______	Date ______
Place ______	Place ______
Male(s) ______ Female(s) ______	Male(s) ______ Female(s) ______
Immature ______ Eclipse ______	Immature ______ Eclipse ______
Behavior Notes	

Mountain Plover

Charadrius montanus 8–9in

Nest Scrape
Egg clutch 3
Egg color Not known
Laid May–June
Incubation 29 days by male alone
Fledging 33 days

Identification Upperparts are pale brown, underparts whitish, washed buff on the breast and flanks. In breeding plumage males and females are similar, with a white forehead and short supercilium extending back to and just behind the eye, neatly set off by a narrow black line from the eye to the bill and a black forecrown. Birds in winter and juvenile plumage lack these prominent head markings but often have a good buffish breast band. Adults can look very plain-faced, the black markings on the head being replaced by a dull, pale brown. Juveniles have a buffish eyebrow rather than white. The yellowish-brown legs are quite long and the bill is black. In flight the species looks long-winged, with a variable narrow wing bar and white fringe to a dark-centered tail. The underwing is conspicuously white.

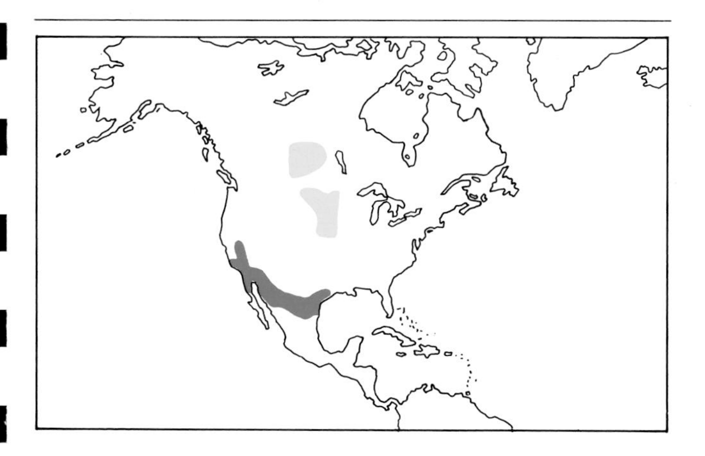

Voice A variety of whistles, including a shrill "kip."
Habitat In breeding season grazes short grass prairies. In winter favors cactus deserts and dry dirt fields.
Food Insects, especially grasshoppers.
Range Breeding area extends from southern Alberta and Saskatchewan south to Montana, and also from central Wyoming south to New Mexico and north-west Texas.
Movements From mid-June onward, birds begin to leave for winter quarters in California and south-west Arizona, extending in a band across northern Mexico to southern Texas. Elsewhere vagrants to Washington, Oregon, Alabama, Florida, Virginia, and Massachusetts.

RECORD OF SIGHTINGS	
Date ______	Date ______
Place ______	Place ______
Male(s) ____ Female(s) ____	Male(s) ____ Female(s) ____
Immature ____ Eclipse ____	Immature ____ Eclipse ____
Behavior Notes	

Bird in winter plumage

Black-bellied Plover

Pluvialis squatarola 10½–12½in

Nest Scrape on mossy lichen-covered ground
Egg clutch 4
Egg color Buffish-gray with darker spotting
Laid End of May to late June in its more northerly limit
Incubation 23 days
Fledging 35–45 days

Identification In summer one of the most strikingly beautiful of shorebirds, its intense black underparts reaching down to the belly. This black area is separated from the silvery-spangled gray and black upperparts by a broad band of pure white. The bill and legs are black. Closely resembling the Golden Plover in its winter colors, it is a somewhat larger and stouter-looking bird, with grayish-white underparts and silver-gray spangling instead of gold on the upperparts. In flight shows a bold white wing bar, white rump and distinctive black axillaries, which identify it immediately.
Voice A mournful, far-carrying "tlee-oo-ee."
Habitat Lowland tundra north of the tree limit in breeding season; mudflats and estuaries in winter.
Food Worms, leather-jackets, and a variety of inter-tidal invertebrates.

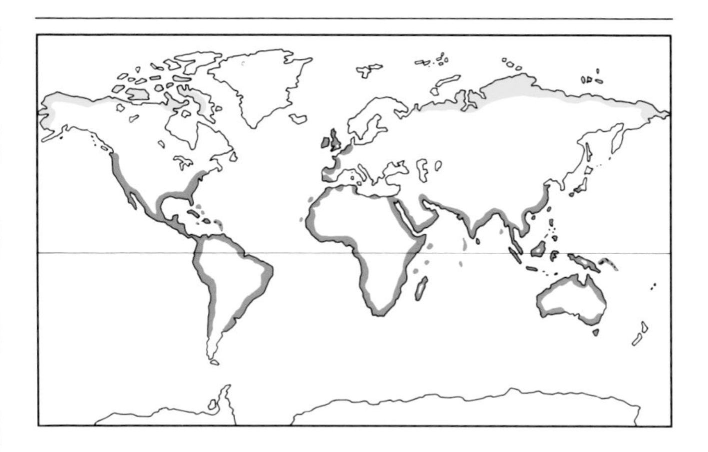

Range Nests almost continuously throughout the entire Arctic region of mainland Russia, Siberia, and North America. Winters in Britain where total population of around 20,000 birds represents about a third of the European population. Also occurs in France, Iberia, and West Africa.

Movements In North America spring passage extends from mid-April to beyond mid-May, generally peaking toward the end of April. In the east birds arrive via the West Indies to points along the Atlantic coast as far as New England, and then generally overland. In the west the tendency is to follow the Pacific coast. The return migration in the fall is probably the spring movement in reverse, with perhaps a more easterly bias.

RECORD OF SIGHTINGS	
Date ______	Date ______
Place ______	Place ______
Male(s) ______ Female(s) ______	Male(s) ______ Female(s) ______
Immature ______ Eclipse ______	Immature ______ Eclipse ______
Behavior Notes	

Bird in winter plumage

American Golden Plover

Pluvialis dominica 9–10in

Nest Scrape in low vegetation
Egg clutch 4
Egg color Buff, boldly spotted and blotched with black
Laid June
Incubation 26 days
Fledging 25–33 days

Identification In summer plumage a very smart-looking bird, with jet-black face, throat, center of chest, belly and undertail coverts forming a continuous and solidly dark underside. The black face extends just over the bill, and above this the prominent white forehead extends with a thick eyebrow. The white blaze envelops the rear ear coverts and then continues to broaden at the sides of the neck to form an oval patch flanking the black of the chest. The upperparts are a mixture of small black, golden and white feathers, giving a spangled effect. In flight the dusky-gray underwing and axiliaries are useful field marks. In winter a rather uniform-looking bird.
Voice Regularly used contact calls are a "chu-wit" and a "tu-ee."
Habitat A true tundra bird, preferring dry gentle slopes with short

vegetation for nesting. In winter inhabits short grassland and tilled agricultural fields, but at times haunts coastal lagoons, mudflats, and inland shallow pools.

Food Invertebrates on breeding grounds, but berries and other vegetable matter taken. Insects and worms are a major food source at other times.

Range Nesting area extends from western Alaska to Baffin Island.

Movements After nesting, they head eastward, which takes them well out into the mid-North Atlantic before they fly due south to central South America. They return northward up the Mississippi, after stopping off on the northern prairies, before continuing their journey.

RECORD OF SIGHTINGS	
Date ______	Date ______
Place ______	Place ______
Male(s) ______ Female(s) ______	Male(s) ______ Female(s) ______
Immature ____ Eclipse ______	Immature ____ Eclipse ______
Behavior Notes	

Bird in breeding plumage

Pacific Golden Plover

Pluvialis fulva 9–10in

Nest Shallow depression in ground, sparsely lined with grass and leaves.
Egg clutch 4, occasionally 5
Egg color Variable cinnamon-buff, with many irregularly scattered dark spots
Laid June
Incubation 27 days
Fledging 28 days

Identification Until recently, this bird and the American Golden Plover were treated as a single species named the Lesser Golden Plover. In breeding plumage both Pacific and American Golden Plovers have predominantly black underparts, but the Pacific has a narrow white line all the way along its flanks from the eyebrow to the undertail, usually broken by black bars on the flanks. Importantly, the Pacific also has largely white undertail coverts. The upperparts are generally more distinctly golden-spangled. In winter the Pacific is essentially yellowish-buff, with bright yellow spangles on the upperparts and a brownish-buff breast, buffish in juveniles, mottled bright yellow in both.
Voice A plaintive "ki-wee" and a "chewit" note reminiscent of a subdued Spotted Redshank's call.
Habitat On breeding territory favors well-drained tundra beyond the tree-line with short sward, moss, and lichen. In winter largely coastal, haunting inter-tidal mud and beaches. Also likes areas of short grass, such as golf courses, playing fields, and salt marshes.

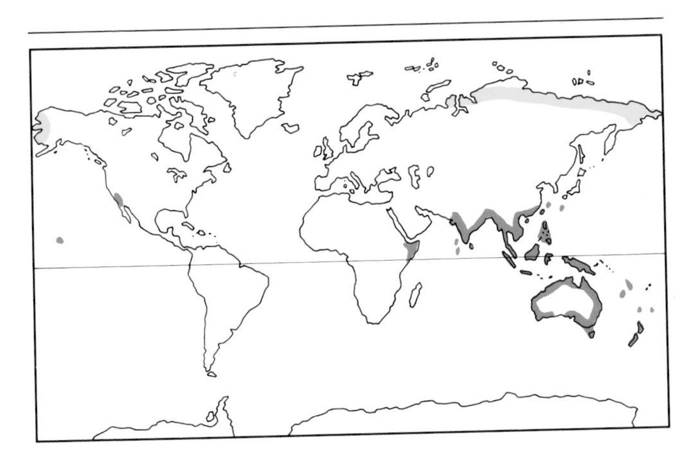

Food A variety of small invertebrates supplemented by berries in the fall.
Range Arctic Siberia from Yamal Peninsula eastward. Also western Alaska and the Bering Sea islands. Winters from north-east Africa around shores of Indian Ocean to south-east Asia, and south to Australia and New Zealand. Birds also reach Pacific Islands. A few are found in southern California.
Movements A prodigious migrant, often traveling enormous distances, for example 3000 miles from Pribilov Islands in Bering Sea to Hawaii. Adults leave breeding grounds July onward, several weeks before juveniles. Return journey starts as early as March but many juveniles spend first summer in winter quarters.

RECORD OF SIGHTINGS	
Date ______	Date ______
Place ______	Place ______
Male(s) ____ Female(s) ____	Male(s) ____ Female(s) ____
Immature ____ Eclipse ____	Immature ____ Eclipse ____
Behavior Notes	

Bird in winter plumage

Marbled Godwit

Limosa fedoa 16–20 in

Nest A depression lined with grass on a raised area in damp ground
Egg clutch 4
Egg color Buff-olive, slightly spotted
Laid May
Incubation 23 days
Fledging 28 days

Identification Largest of the godwits, the breeding plumage, if not strikingly bright, has a warm subtle beauty with dark brown and black upperparts heavily spotted and streaked with buff, white, and chestnut. These give a marbled effect, hence its name. The underparts are tawny brown barred darker brown on the neck base and flanks. In winter there is no great change in color but it looks paler and plainer. At all times the conspicuously cinnamon flight feathers contrasting with dark outer primaries are a feature of this bird. Juveniles are like non-breeding adults. The long, slightly upturned pink and black bill and dark legs, which project beyond the tail when on the wing, should further help put a name to this less dramatically plumaged godwit.
Voice Noisy on breeding ground, where it utters a distinctive hoarse "kerrek." Alarm note in contrast a "wik-wik."
Habitat Prairie wetlands close to ponds, streams, fresh or saline lakes for breeding. At other times found on estuaries, beaches, flooded fields, and marshes.
Food Molluscs, crustaceans, worms, leeches, larval insects.

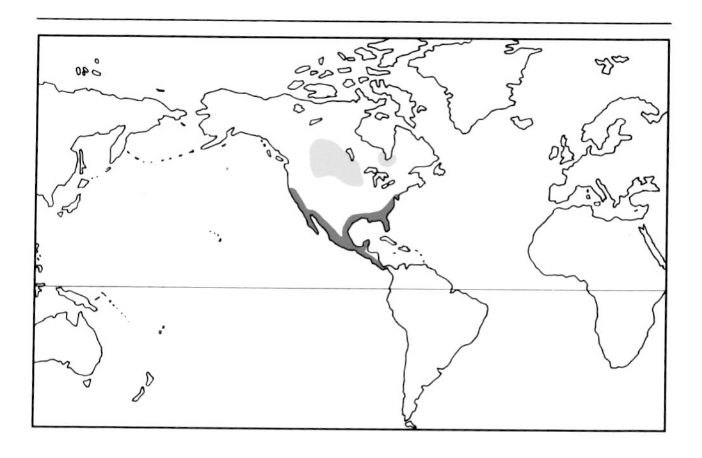

Range Canadian central prairie provinces to Montana, North and South Dakota and western Minnesota for nesting. Formerly nested in Nebraska, Iowa and Wisconsin, but numbers have declined markedly in recent decades. During winter the vast majority of the population is found on the Pacific coast of California through to Mexico and Panama. Others frequent the Gulf coast south to Central America.

Movements A relatively short-distance migrant, birds return early and are on the breeding grounds by May. After nesting, the males form into large pre-migratory flocks. By the end of July, birds are heading south-west to the California coast, with smaller numbers flying south-east to the Gulf of Mexico.

RECORD OF SIGHTINGS	
Date ______	Date ______
Place ______	Place ______
Male(s) ______ Female(s) ______	Male(s) ______ Female(s) ______
Immature ______ Eclipse ______	Immature ______ Eclipse ______
Behavior Notes	

Bird in breeding plumage

Hudsonian Godwit

Limosa haemastica 14–16 in

Nest Depression in grass tussock lined with grass and dried leaves
Egg clutch 4
Egg color Olive-buff, sparingly spotted with dark markings
Laid June
Incubation 22–25 day
Fledging Around 30 days

Identification In breeding plumage has deep chestnut red-brown and red belly, light gray head and neck, which contrast markedly with the black and yellow-spangled back, giving the bird a very regal look. The long orange bill with a black tip is slightly upturned, while the longish legs are dark gray. Normally shy and easily disturbed, it takes flight, revealing narrow white wing bars, a black and white tail, and protruding legs. At such times it bears some resemblance to the European Black-tailed Godwit, but is more slender-looking, with less extensive areas of white on the wings and tail. In winter plumage, however, both species look similar with grayish upperparts and a white breast underneath, but the Hudsonian Godwit has only to raise its wings, revealing the jet black linings, to dispel any doubt as to its identify.
Voice A modulating trill reminiscent of the Whimbrel.
Habitat For nesting chooses sedge marshes, bogs, and meadows in

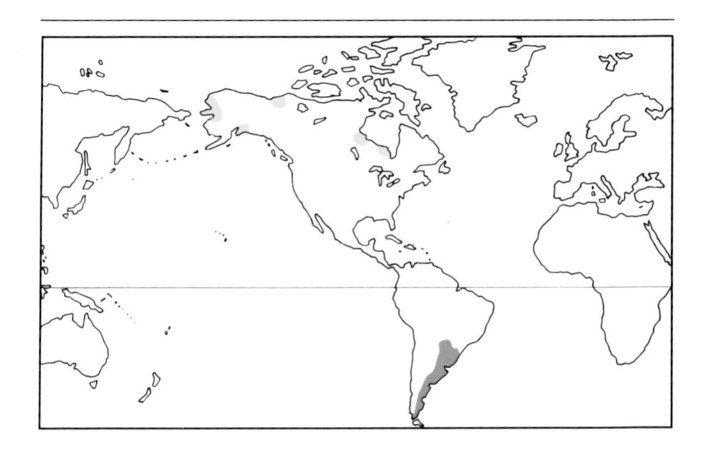

the vicinity of lakes and the coast at the edge of the tree-line. At other times chooses a variety of aquatic habitats, from estuaries and tidal beaches to freshwater and saline lagoons.

Food Worms, molluscs, and crustaceans.

Range Breeds in north-western British Columbia, parts of Alaska and northern Canada from the Mackenzie rift valley to Hudson Bay. Winters in Argentina south to Tierra del Fuego.

Movements Makes brief stops on spring passage as it moves quickly north through the Great Lakes. From the end of July birds mass on the east Canadian coast around St James' Bay and Hudson Bay areas, where almost the entire population of this species passes through prior to their flight south.

RECORD OF SIGHTINGS	
Date ______	Date ______
Place ______	Place ______
Male(s) ______ Female(s) ______	Male(s) ______ Female(s) ______
Immature ______ Eclipse ______	Immature ______ Eclipse ______
Behavior Notes	

Bird in breeding plumage

Whimbrel

Numenius phaeopus 16–18½ in

Nest	Scrape on short tussocky vegetation
Egg clutch	4
Egg color	Olive brown, spotted and blotched brown and lavender
Laid	May–June
Incubation	27–28 days
Fledging	35–42 days

Identification The combination of a pale buff central stripe and eyebrows contrasting strongly with darker sides to the crown and eyestripe, are particularly distinctive. The upperparts are dark brown, with variably marked pale feather fringes, giving a more mottled appearance at a distance. In flight the brown lower back and rump of *Numenius p. hudsonica,* which is the usual race occurring in North America, can be seen to be uniform with the rest of the upperparts. (In the nominate race, *Numenius p. phaeopus*, these areas are contrastingly white.) The underparts are buffish-white variably streaked with darker brown on the breast. Juveniles look similar to adults but the crown is darker, showing less contrast with the lateral crown stripes and eyebrows.

Voice A rapid tittering "titti, titti, titti, titti, titti, titti, titti" of even emphasis. Song is a babbling trill.

Habitat Open tundra or comparatively dry moorland. In winter haunts mudflats, beaches, and estuaries.

Food Has a wide diet; generally includes molluscs, crustaceans, and annelids or snails, beetles and earthworms, as available. Seeds and berries are also taken at times.

Range Virtually circumpolar as a breeding bird. Icelandic, north European and central Siberian nesting birds winter in the Afrotropics and along the west coasts of the Indian Ocean. Those

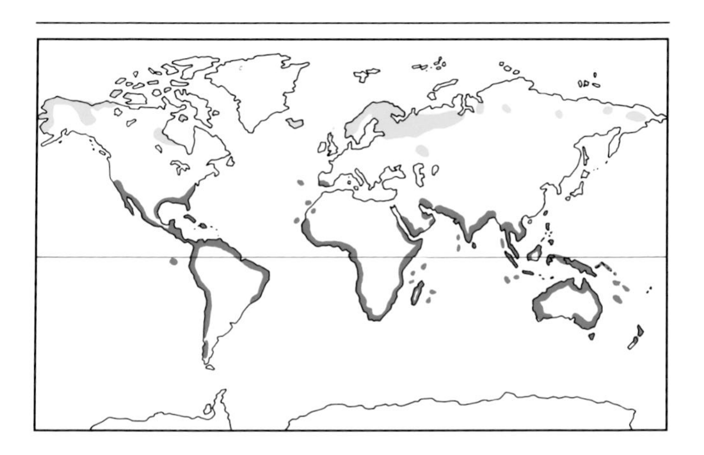

that nest further east are to be found in south-east Asia and Australasia. Alaskan breeders winter along coasts of South America, as far south as Tierra del Fuego.

Movements Birds move up the Pacific coast in spring but can also be seen locally inland, passing through the interior. The fall route is the reverse of this. On the Atlantic side birds arrive via the West Indies, generally migrating along the coast up to Chesapeake Bay, sometimes as far as New Jersey, then inland to St James' Bay and West Hudson Bay. In the fall some birds cross the Ungava Peninsula to the outer part of the Gulf of St Lawrence; others cross from St James' Bay to the Gulf, then all follow the same course to the maritimes. From there they fly over water to the New Jersey area to continue the spring route in reverse.

RECORD OF SIGHTINGS	
Date ______	Date ______
Place ______	Place ______
Male(s) ______ Female(s) ______	Male(s) ______ Female(s) ______
Immature ______ Eclipse ______	Immature ______ Eclipse ______
Behavior Notes	

Long-billed Curlew

Numenius americana 20–26 in

Nest	A hollow depression in grass
Egg clutch	4
Egg color	Whitish-buff to deep olive, with spots and blotches of brown
Laid	May/June
Incubation	30 days
Fledging	About 6 weeks

Identification The largest North American shorebird, the long curved bill can vary in size from twice the head-length in some males and most juveniles, to three times the head-length in females. In summer the drab brownish plumage becomes a buffy-orange. The head is small and gray and almost unmarked, except for an inconspicuous white eyebrow. The long thin neck, breast and belly are a bright orangy-buff color with fine dark streakings and spots. The mantle and wing coverts are black, uniformly spangled with buff and orange. The body plumage color is further enhanced by bright orange underwing linings and axillaries which are prominent in flight. Additionally, the darker coverts and outer primaries contrast markedly with the bright orange trailing edge of the long wings.

Voice An eerie echoing "cour-lee."

Habitat Prairie and rolling grassland for nesting; at other times mudflats, estuaries, saline and freshwater lakes, flooded fields, etc.

Food Worms, crustaceans, crabs, small fish, amphibians, insect larvae. On the nesting grounds berries and insects are taken.

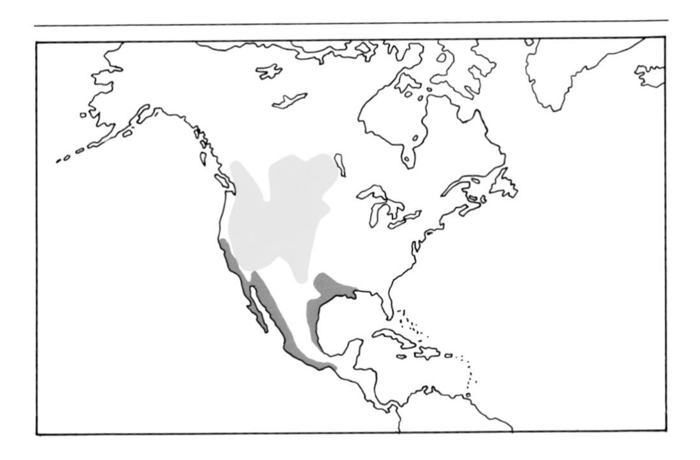

Range As a breeding bird, confined to south-west and southern Canada, California, Utah, Nevada, northern New Mexico, and coastal and northern Texas. Within this area, two races of Long-billed Curlew are now recognized. The "Lesser" Long-billed Curlew and the "Greater" Long-billed — each race breeding in a different part of the above area. During winter found in Mexico, Guatemala, Venezuela, and Panama.

Movements Birds return to their nesting territories by the end of April. After nesting at the beginning of July the females vacate the breeding areas. About six weeks later the males and juveniles move to the coasts of California, South Carolina and Texas, and by October are making their way southward to winter quarters.

RECORD OF SIGHTINGS	
Date ________	Date ________
Place ________	Place ________
Male(s) ____ Female(s) ____	Male(s) ____ Female(s) ____
Immature ____ Eclipse ____	Immature ____ Eclipse ____
Behavior Notes	

Willet

Catoptrophorus semipalmatus 13–16½ in

Nest A hollow in long grass, but sometimes in open
Egg clutch 4
Egg color Olive-buff, evenly blotched with brown
Laid May
Incubation 21–29 days
Fledging 14–15 days

Identification The upperparts, including the nape, mantle, scapulars, and wing coverts, are light to brownish-gray, with fine white edgings on all feathers. The expressionless face is finely streaked with gray with a bold white ring around the eye joined to the base of the bill by a white loral stripe, giving the effect of a pair of white spectacles when viewed front-on. The breast is plain gray and the belly white. The bill is medium sized and stout, while the long legs are blue-gray. There are two separate breeding populations, the Western (or Inland) Willet and the Eastern Willet, which vary in breeding plumage. The Eastern Willet has a boldly-barred and brown-spotted neck, breast and flanks, while the Western Willet has a plain, liberally-streaked breast. The two have similar underparts, which are gray-brown barred buff with dark brown. In any plumage this bird is immediately identifiable in flight. The black primaries and coverts with a broad white lateral bar are distinctive, while the black linings of the underwing axillaries and primary tips contrast with the translucent white secondaries. The white rump, finely barred tail and projecting legs further aid identification.
Voice A loud shrieking "kip-kip."
Habitat Nests in marshy areas. Outside breeding season favors mudflats and tidal estuaries.

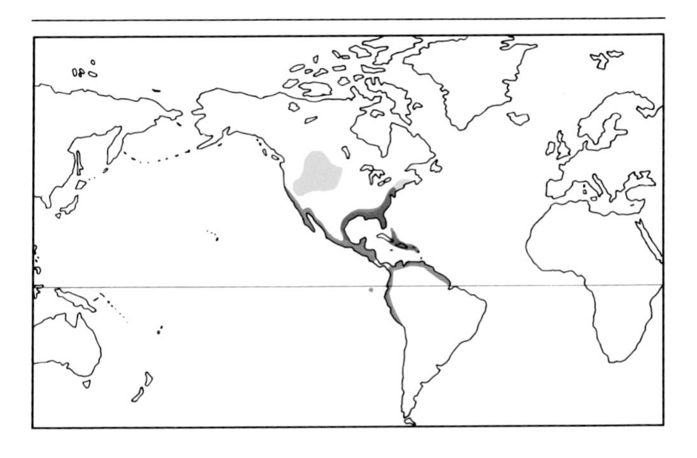

Food Freshwater and marine invertebrates, some vegetable matter.
Range In breeding season the Western Willet is confined to the prairies and central southern Canada, including northern California, Oregon, Idaho, Alberta, North and South Dakota, Nebraska, and Colorado. The Eastern Willet is to be found in a continuous strip along the Atlantic seaboard from Nova Scotia southward to Florida, then westward along the Gulf to the coast of Texas. The Western Willet winters in southern California, Peru, and the Galapagos. The Eastern Willet is more sedentary over much of its range.
Movements Migrating birds arrive in the southern USA mid-March, and reach breeding areas by May. After nesting dispersal, the adults leave early August and juveniles follow a few weeks later.

RECORD OF SIGHTINGS	
Date ______	Date ______
Place ______	Place ______
Male(s) ______ Female(s) ______	Male(s) ______ Female(s) ______
Immature ______ Eclipse ______	Immature ______ Eclipse ______
Behavior Notes	

Bird in breeding plumage

Greater Yellowlegs

Tringa melanoleuca 13–15 in

Nest A hollow lined with dry vegetation
Egg clutch 4
Egg color Buffish or greenish, blotched with chestnut and darker browns
Laid May/June
Incubation 24 days
Fledging 28 days

Identification A large, robust version of the commoner Lesser Yellowlegs, the upperparts are generally dark brown, with various lighter markings, including many small white flecks. The underparts are white, streaked dark on the neck and breast, with barring on the sides. The bright yellow legs, which give the bird its name, are brighter than Lesser Yellowlegs, while the bill is long and slightly upcurved. The ratio of head to bill is a useful guide to identification, the Greater Yellowleg's bill being one and a half times as long as the head and somewhat broader at the base. In flight there is a square white rump. The sexes are similar.
Voice Flight call is "chu, chu, chu, chu."
Habitat In breeding season open areas among tall woodland with sparse undergrowth, interspersed with marshy pools. At other times

tidal beaches, mudflats, lagoons, flooded fields, and similar water locations.

Food Worms, insect larvae, crustaceans, snails, and at times grasshoppers.

Range Breeds in southern Alaska through British Columbia eastward to Newfoundland and extending northward to sub-Arctic tundra. Some winter in the southern states of the USA, but most move to the West Indies and South America.

Movements By the middle of May, birds reach their breeding grounds. After nesting, some birds are on their way south again at the end of July. Throughout August its passage is in full swing. By mid-October most birds have cleared the USA.

RECORD OF SIGHTINGS	
Date ______	Date ______
Place ______	Place ______
Male(s) ____ Female(s) ____	Male(s) ____ Female(s) ____
Immature ____ Eclipse ____	Immature ____ Eclipse ____
Behavior Notes	

Bird in breeding plumage

Lesser Yellowlegs

Tringa flavipes 9½–11 in

Nest	Hollow beneath bush or small tree lined with grass and leaves
Egg clutch	4
Egg color	Olive to creamy-buff, evenly spotted with dark red
Laid	June
Incubation	22 days
Fledging	23–25 days

Identification A medium-sized, slender, almost dainty-looking bird, with long bright yellow legs. It is dark brown on the back and coverts, which are spotted and edged with white. The head, neck and upper breast are white and heavily streaked with gray, while the rest of the underparts are white and clean. In flight a square white rump is the most obvious feature, with disproportionately long wings, a gray and white barred tail and projecting legs. On its own, a very confiding and approachable bird, nervously bobbing its head and tail. The long, slender bill is a major difference from the Greater Yellowlegs.
Voice A loud piercing "kip, kip" on breeding grounds. Has a "tew-tew" flight call.
Habitat For nesting chooses either hilly or flattish ground in the northern forest zone among trees with little undergrowth, wherever marshes and muskegs are close at hand. At other times coastal beaches, mudflats, brackish lagoons, freshwater lakes and pools; especially fond of flooded fields.

Food Crustaceans, small fish, insects and their larvae, and small aquatic life.
Range Nests in north central Alaska and adjacent Canadian provinces, including the Yukon, stretching southward through the prairies and eastward to northern Ontario and western Quebec. Winters in the West Indies, Chile, and Argentina.
Movements In spring spreads northward on a broad front, but generally more numerous east of the Rockies, and has a tendency to concentrate in the eastern and Gulf States. Main route takes them through the Mississippi valley northward to the Great Lakes, where the birds fan out in a north and north-westerly direction. The fall return is concentrated along the Atlantic seaboard.

RECORD OF SIGHTINGS	
Date ________	Date ________
Place ________	Place ________
Male(s) ____ Female(s) ____	Male(s) ____ Female(s) ____
Immature ____ Eclipse ____	Immature ____ Eclipse ____
Behavior Notes	

Bird in breeding plumage

Solitary Sandpiper

Tringa solitaria 7–8½ in

Nest Occupies the disused nest of a small passerine
Egg clutch 4
Egg color Greenish or creamy-buff, spotted and blotched brown
Laid Late May–early June
Incubation Probably around 21 days
Fledging Probaby around 28 days

Identification A medium-sized wader with bill and legs neither exceptionally short nor long. The adult has blackish-brown upperparts, slightly paler and more olive on the head and neck, and finely speckled with white and buff. The breast is grayish-white and heavily streaked with dark brown, the streaking extending to the flanks; the rest of the underparts are white. In non-breeding plumage is a little paler and grayer, with rather less spotting, while the juvenile is similar to the summer adult, but a bit browner with buffer spotting. In all plumages the legs are gray-green and the bill blackish with an olive base. There is a prominent white eye-ring and a short stripe extending from the bill to the eye. In flight shows dark wings and a dark rump and tail. There is some barring to the sides of the tail.
Voice Normally a thin weak "pip" or "pip-pip." In full flight

utters a "pleet-weet-weet," sharper than Spotted Sandpiper.
Habitat In breeding season found in open coniferous forest in the vicinity of water. On passage can turn up beside any patch of water. In winter frequents rivers and edges of lakes and ponds, also coastal mangroves.
Food Insects, small crustaceans, spiders, and small frogs.
Range Breeds from Alaska across Canada to Labrador, north to the tree-line and south to a line from central British Columbia to central Ontario.
Movements In spring passes through USA in April and early May. First returning birds are noted in late June, though bulk of passage is from mid-August to September.

RECORD OF SIGHTINGS	
Date ______	Date ______
Place ______	Place ______
Male(s) ______ Female(s) ______	Male(s) ______ Female(s) ______
Immature ______ Eclipse ______	Immature ______ Eclipse ______
Behavior Notes	

Bird in breeding plumage

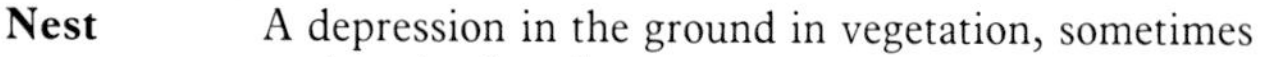

Spotted Sandpiper

Actitus macularia 7–8 in

Nest A depression in the ground in vegetation, sometimes under a bush or log
Egg clutch 4
Egg color Buff, heavily spotted and blotched with brown
Laid May/June
Incubation 20–21 days
Fledging 13–16 days

Identification In breeding plumage this small sandpiper is most distinctive with its spotted underparts. Also noticeable are the numerous black cross-bars on the olive brown upperparts. There is a whitish supercilium and the base of the shortish bill is pinkish. The legs are orange-yellow or pinkish. In winter it shows relatively pale unmarked olive or gray-brown upperparts, with all white underparts and yellowish legs. There is a dark patch at the side of the neck and between this and the bend of the wing a very distinctive white shoulder mark. Its teetering bobbing gait is most characteristic, as is its flight, which is low over the water with flickering wingbeats interspersed with frequent glides. There are short narrow wing bars and the tail and rump are unmarked.
Voice In flight gives a shrill "peet-weet" or a "weet-weet-weet." Sometimes a quiet "pit" note is uttered.
Habitat Most waterside conditions from sea level to the tree-line

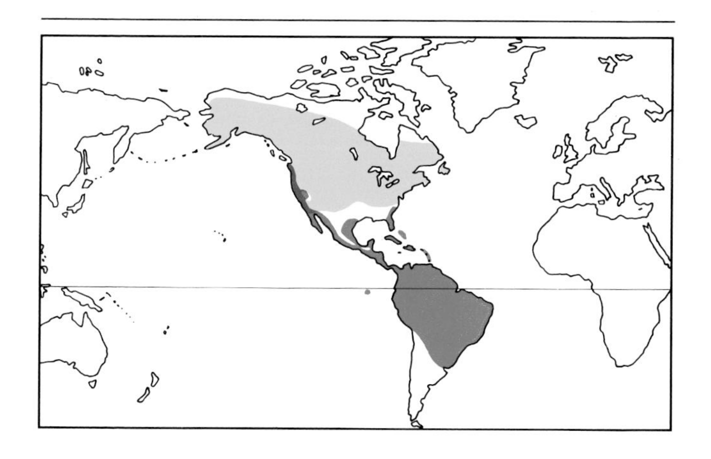

suit it for nesting, though sometimes found well away from water. Often chooses farmland or pastures. At other times shores of lakes, creeks, lagoons, flooded fields, marshy areas. Shuns the open shore.
Food Insects and a range of freshwater invertebrates.
Range Breeds across North America from Alaska to Newfoundland, and south to southern California, North Carolina and Maryland. Winters in west from British Columbia, southward and east from the Carolinas to Argentina and Peru.
Movements Birds pass northward through USA in early April to June on a broad front, often at night. Usually, only lone birds encountered. Return passage after breeding begins early August, continuing through to early October.

RECORD OF SIGHTINGS	
Date ______	Date ______
Place ______	Place ______
Male(s) ______ Female(s) ______	Male(s) ______ Female(s) ______
Immature ______ Eclipse ______	Immature ______ Eclipse ______
Behavior Notes	

Bird in breeding plumage

Wandering Tattler

Heteroscelus incanus 10–11½ in

Nest A depression in the ground sometimes lined with roots and twigs
Egg clutch 4
Egg color Greenish, spotted and blotched with brown
Laid May/June
Incubation 23–25 days
Fledging Unknown

Identification A stocky, short-legged bird, it is mainly slate-gray in all plumages. In breeding plumage adults are gray above, with a short, narrow whitish supercilium and, most notably, gray barring over all the underparts, including the undertail coverts. The bill is black, with a variable greenish bar, and the legs are yellow. In winter and juvenile plumage there is no barring on the underparts but there is a dark gray wash over the breast and flanks. The juvenile also has very fine pale fringes to the feathers of the upperparts. In flight shows no distinctive markings. Best distinguished from similar Gray-tailed Tattler by call.
Voice A distinctive rippling trill, a rapid accelerated series of hollow whistles all on the same pitch. (The very similar-looking Gray-tailed Tattler's call is a "too-weet," reminiscent of American Golden Plover.)

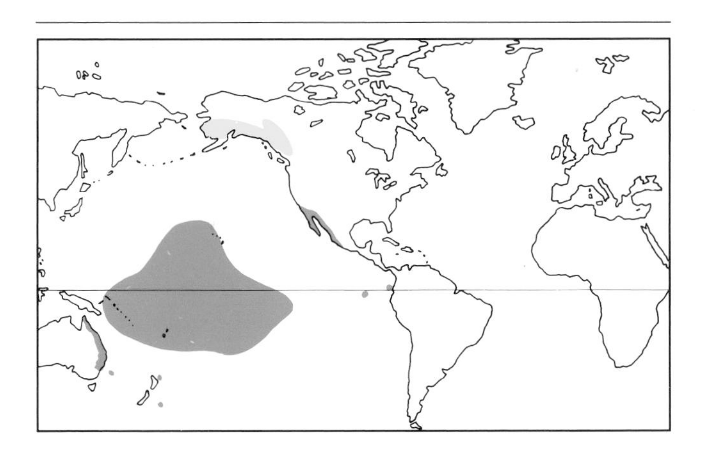

Habitat In breeding season favors the alpine zone of mountains and highland nesting on islands in fast-flowing, gravel-bottomed streams. On passage and in winter haunts rocky coasts and reefs, also nearby sand and shingle beaches. Found at times along the shores of ponds, well away from salt water.
Food Mainly caddisfly and their larvae when on breeding grounds. At other times crustaceans, worms, and molluscs.
Range Breeds in areas of south coastal, central and western Alaska, east to the Yukon and British Columbia. Also probably breeds in far eastern Siberia. Winters from southern California south to Ecuador, and also on the Galapagos and Hawaiian Islands, and on the islands of the central and south Pacific west to the Great Barrier Reef and northern New Zealand.

RECORD OF SIGHTINGS	
Date ______	Date ______
Place ______	Place ______
Male(s) ____ Female(s) ____	Male(s) ____ Female(s) ____
Immature ____ Eclipse ____	Immature ____ Eclipse ____
Behavior Notes	

Wilson's Phalarope

Phalaropus tricolor 8½–9½ in

Nest A scrape in long grass
Egg clutch 4
Egg color Yellowish, heavily spotted with black
Laid June
Incubation 16–21 days
Fledging No reliable information

Identification Largest of the phalaropes, it shows a disproportionately bulky body, a long slender neck and small rounded head. Additionally, the shortish legs are placed well back on its body, giving a top-heavy, pot-bellied look. As with other phalaropes, the female is more brightly colored, and in breeding plumage shows a strikingly pronounced thick, black patch extending from the base of her bill through the face, then down the side of the neck, separating the bright white throat, chestnut foreneck and upper breast from the pearl-gray crown, hindneck and nape. In winter sexes are alike, being pale gray-brown above and white below. Sometimes there is a dark mark through the eye. The black bill is long and needle-fine, and the legs are yellowish (black in summer plumage). In flight shows dark wings and white rump. When feeding in shallow water "spins" characteristically. Less aquatic than other phalaropes.
Voice A nasal grunting "aangh." Also has a flight call "chu."
Habitat In breeding season found on prairie wetland meadows; at other times inland lakes and pools.
Food Spiders, beetles, crustaceans, insects, seeds are also taken.
Range Breeds in north-west, north central and middle USA and Canada, covering at least 16 states from Manitoba south to central California, stretching to Kansas then north-east to the Great Lakes. In Canada its expanding range now extends from British Columbia to Ontario. Winters entirely on inland lakes and pools of the

Argentinian and Chilean pampas, and at high-altitude lakes in Peru. **Movements** In spring migration is generally noted inland with a westerly bias, though a few birds are to be seen east of the Mississippi. Birds reach the breeding grounds by mid-May. Shortly after the eggs are laid, females abandon nest-site, gathering together in large flocks on nearby pools before departing southward in late June. Males and young leave middle of August. Movement is prolonged, with birds lingering at favorable areas as they take an inland route through the western states of the USA, across the inner part of the Gulf of Mexico and the Isthmus of Tehuantepec, then over the Pacific toward Ecuador and the more southerly areas of South America.

RECORD OF SIGHTINGS	
Date ______	Date ______
Place ______	Place ______
Male(s) ______ Female(s) ______	Male(s) ______ Female(s) ______
Immature ______ Eclipse ______	Immature ______ Eclipse ______
Behavior Notes	

Bird in winter plumage

Red-necked Phalarope

Phalaropus lobatus 7–7½ in

Nest A scrape lined with leaves and grass stems
Egg clutch 4
Egg color Buffy-olive, blotched with dark brown
Laid June
Incubation 21 days
Fledging About 21 days

Identification The size of a Dunlin, this is the smallest of the phalaropes, with a slim neck, small oval head and long needle-fine bill, giving it an overall slender and elegant appearance. The breeding female has a slate-gray head, neck and back, with buff edgings to the scapulars and mantle, brownish wings, a white throat and belly and a gray breast band. The most distinctive feature, however, is the orange-red horseshoe mark on the neck. The male is similarly patterned, but much duller and more diffuse, with browner upperparts, a paler orange neck and a less distinctive neck band. Winter adults can easily be confused with gray/Red Phalaropes. Juveniles can be distinguished by a brownish-black cap and dark brown upperparts with buff margins to the mantle and scapulars. Their white underparts have a buffish suffusion.
Voice A "whit" or "prip" similar to Red Phalarope but lower-pitched.
Habitat Breeds around coasts and near inland pools, particularly where there is emergent vegetation. Marshy ground with tiny pools and watercourses set among rich lowland vegetation is also favored. On migration will stop off and feed on any lake or pool, no matter how small. At other times on seashore and way out on the oceans.
Food On the breeding ground eats chironomid midges especially, and other small insects and their larvae. Its most characteristic

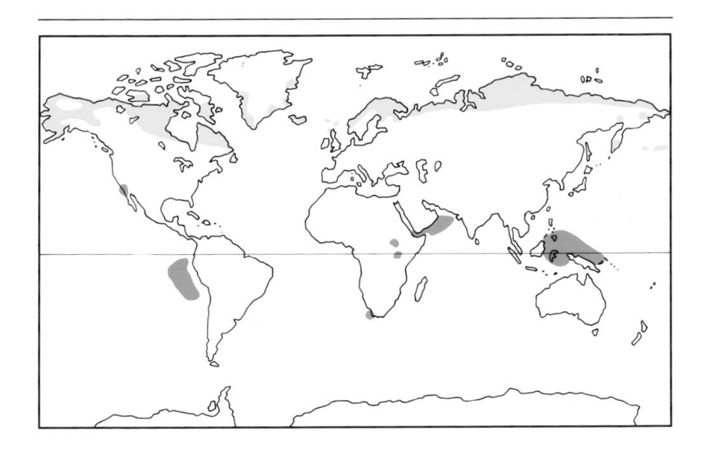

means of taking such food is from the water's surface while "spinning."

Range Breeds right across the Holarctic region but winters in warmer latitudes, principally off Peru, in the Arabian Sea and around the East Indies.

Movements Northward migration is late, occurring between April and early June. Almost immediately after the eggs hatch some females begin their return south, unless they take up with another male and lay a second clutch. Males start their journey south in July. The young follow in August and early September.

RECORD OF SIGHTINGS	
Date ______	Date ______
Place ______	Place ______
Male(s) ______ Female(s) ______	Male(s) ______ Female(s) ______
Immature ______ Eclipse ______	Immature ______ Eclipse ______
Behavior Notes	

Female in breeding plumage

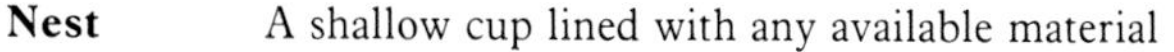

Red Phalarope

Phalaropus fulicaria 8–8½ in

Nest A shallow cup lined with any available material
Egg clutch 4
Egg color Olive, with dark spots and blotches
Laid June
Incubation 21 days
Fledging 14–15 days

Identification Quite unmistakable in breeding plumage, having prominent white cheeks, rich chestnut underparts, blackish-brown back with pale buff feather edgings and a black-tipped yellow bill. Females can have an unstreaked black-brown chin, crown and hindneck. The male is similar but duller and more mottled. They have streaking on the crown, dingier cheeks and drabber underparts, often with some white on the belly. However, the plumage differences between breeding male and females is less marked than in the other two species of phalaropes. The short-lived juvenile plumage suggests a washed-out adult. In winter the plumage is basically white, except for a blackish-gray crown that extends some way on the hindneck, a pale gray back and a blackish mark through and behind the eye. The bill is thicker and broader, the head is bigger and the neck is thicker. On the water it swims with its back horizontal and the tail held higher. In flight shows longer, broader wings than the Red-necked Phalarope, though wing bars are less obvious than in that species.
Voice Usual call a whistling "wit."
Habitat In breeding season favors marshy tundra surrounding Arctic coasts and islands, usually where there are pools with muddy shorelines. In winter almost entirely oceanic.

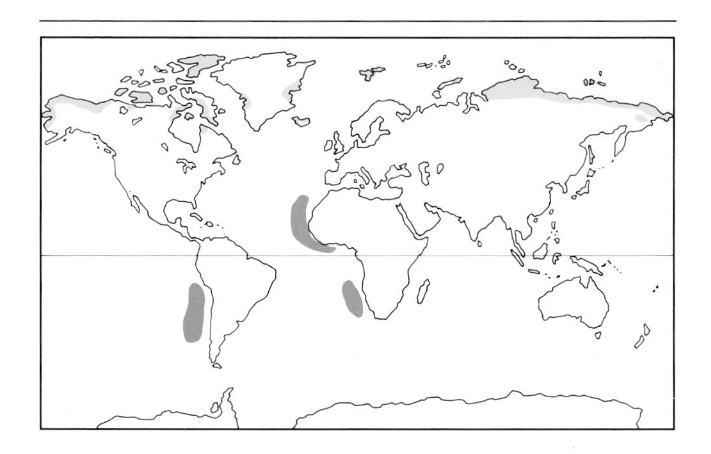

Food Insect larvae, crustacean, insects, vegetable matter, and seeds. Out at sea eats various planktonic fare.

Range Breeds discontinuously around the Arctic Circle. Main wintering grounds are off the coasts of West and South Africa and Chile; some birds remain as far north as the North Sea.

Movements Birds leave wintering area between February and April and reach the edge of the pack-ice in late May or June. After the young hatch, females leave in first half of July, with males and juveniles following in late July and August. Most numerous along the Pacific seaboard where most are seen between September and December.

RECORD OF SIGHTINGS	
Date ________	Date ________
Place ________	Place ________
Male(s) ____ Female(s) ____	Male(s) ____ Female(s) ____
Immature ____ Eclipse ____	Immature ____ Eclipse ____
Behavior Notes	

Female in breeding plumage

Short-billed Dowitcher

Limnodromus griseus 9½–11½ in

Nest A well-hidden depression lined with grass or moss
Egg clutch 4
Egg color Olive-buff, spotted with brown
Laid June
Incubation 21 days
Fledging About 21 days

Identification A medium-sized, stocky shorebird with long snipe-like bill and relatively short legs. Feeds on open mud or shallow water with head-down, distinctive sewing machine-like action. In breeding plumage rusty orange-red below and a mixture of black, buff, and rufous above. Some have a white belly, a feature never shown by Long-billed Dowitcher in summer plumage. In flight has a distinctive shape, with a plump body and comparatively narrow wings, as well as a long, straight bill. There is a lozenge-shaped white wedge on the rump and lower back, and the tail is barred dark and white, appearing gray at a distance. In winter looks dull gray above and white below, washed gray on breast and flanks, with a distinct white supercilium. Juveniles have underparts and head washed with buff, and the feathers of the crown and upperparts have broad orange-buff fringes and irregular orange markings within dark centers, notably on "tiger-striped" tertials.
Voice A mellow "tu-tu-tu," recalling a Lesser Yellowlegs.
Habitat Swamps and open marshes, quaking bogs with low scrub, and sometimes swampy coastal tundra, are used for nesting. At other times can be found in a wide variety of wetlands inland and along the coast.
Food Various marine invertebrates, earthworms, flies and their larvae, also seeds of aquatic plants.
Range Breeds in three distinct areas of northern North America: eastern Canada (northern Quebec), northern Canada (eastern

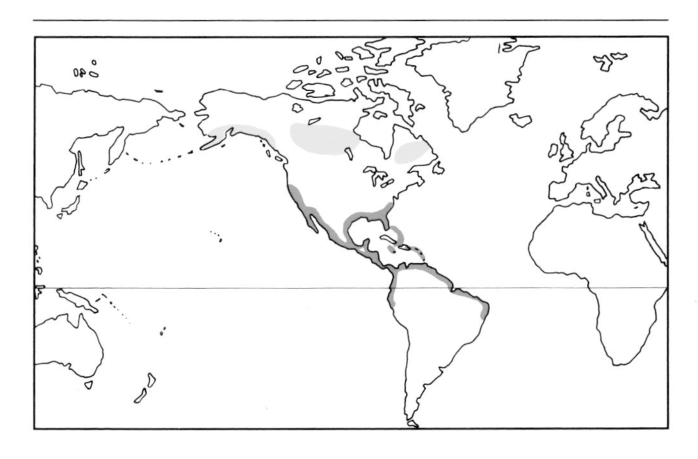

British Columbia, northern Alberta, Saskatchewan and Manitoba), and southern Alaska. Breeding Alaskan birds winter on the coast from California south to Peru (some more inland in the western States). Central Canadian birds winter on the Gulf coast and both east and west coasts of Central America, as far south as Panama; some move to the Atlantic coast from Long Island southward. Those from Quebec winter from North Carolina to Florida, and around the shores of the Caribbean and South America to Brazil. **Movements** In spring birds pass through the USA from early March to early June. After the young hatch, females may leave as early as end of June. Males follow a few weeks later. The juveniles form a third migration peak from July onward.

RECORD OF SIGHTINGS	
Date ______	Date ______
Place ______	Place ______
Male(s) ______ Female(s) ______	Male(s) ______ Female(s) ______
Immature ____ Eclipse ______	Immature ____ Eclipse ______
Behavior Notes	

Moulting into breeding plumage

Long-billed Dowitcher

Limnodromus scolopaceus 10½–12 in

Nest A well-hidden depression lined with grass or moss
Egg clutch 4
Egg color Olive-buff spotted with brown
Laid June
Incubation 21 days
Fledging About 21 days

Identification Very similar in appearance to the Short-billed Dowitcher. In summer plumage the orangy-red is a much deeper shade, while the foreneck is spotted brown and the breast is spotted and barred — otherwise similar and requires ideal viewing conditions to ascertain the more subtle differences (see Short-billed Dowitcher). However, the juvenile plumages of the two can be readily distinguished, as Long-billed Dowitchers are washed with buff below, often with a distinctly grayer head and neck, while the upperparts show narrow rusty fringes and solidly dark centers.
Voice The best distinguishing feature, being a shrill, slightly oystercatcher-like "keek," sometimes in an excited series when alarmed.
Habitat Breeding area is tundra beyond the tree-line in grassy or sedgy swamps, often near a small lake. At other times prefers fresh water or brackish pools to inter-tidal mud.
Food Various freshwater molluscs, earthworms, flies and fly larvae, plus marine invertebrates and seeds.
Range Breeds along the north-east coast of Siberia from the Chukotskiy Peninsula west to Van Karem Bay, and in the Anadyr basin. In North America breeds on St Lawrence Island and coastal

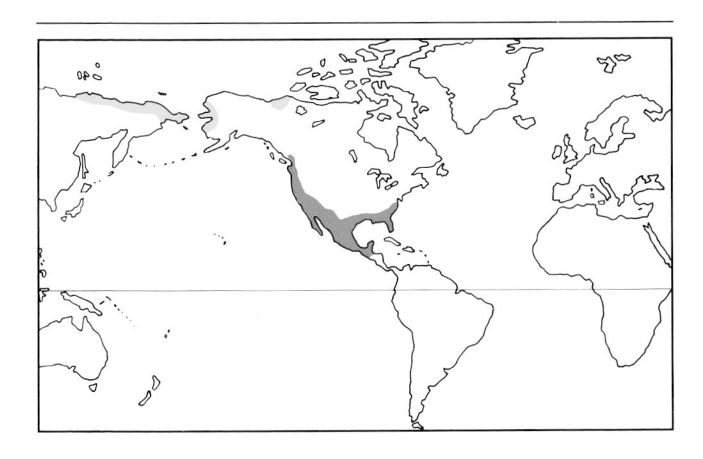

and western Alaska, and probably north-west Mackenzie and the northern Yukon. Wintering grounds in southern USA extend from South Carolina and Florida west to central California, then south through Mexico to Panama.

Movements On spring passage moves north at end of March through to mid-May but rare on Atlantic coast at that time, mostly occurring to the west of the Mississippi. Arrives on breeding ground in late May (June in Siberia). Females begin return migration late June. Males who tend young leave late July or early August. Because of its more distant breeding grounds, usually passes through the USA on a schedule five to six weeks behind the Short-billed Dowitcher.

RECORD OF SIGHTINGS	
Date ______	Date ______
Place ______	Place ______
Male(s) ______ Female(s) ______	Male(s) ______ Female(s) ______
Immature ______ Eclipse ______	Immature ______ Eclipse ______
Behavior Notes	

In winter plumage

Stilt Sandpiper

Micropalama himantopus 7–8 in

Nest A rudimentary depression, often well exposed
Egg clutch 4
Egg color Buff flecked with brown
Incubation 20 days
Fledging 17–18 days

Identification Non-breeding birds look mainly grayish at a distance, but closer views reveal white fringes to the feathers on upperparts, and a distinct white supercilium contrasting with darker lores and crown. The underparts are whitish, with fine, darker gray streaking on the breast and flanks. From March birds moult into distinctive breeding dress, with a dark barred lower breast and belly, and dark streaked neck. The black feathers of the upperparts show rufous and white borders. The white supercilium is even more conspicuous, contrasting strongly with a darker crown, warm chestnut lores, ear coverts, and nape. The legs are rather long, as the name suggests, and these are ocher yellow. The longish bill is marginally thicker and only slightly decurved compared with the Curlew Sandpiper. In flight shows little trace of a wing bar, the gray-brown of the wing contrasting with the whole upper tail coverts, which are square cut in line with the trailing edge of the wings. Juveniles resemble winter adults but show a darker crown and more prominent white supercilium.
Voice A soft trilled "krrr" or "srrrt."
Habitat Mainly dry tundra for nesting, but at other times shows a

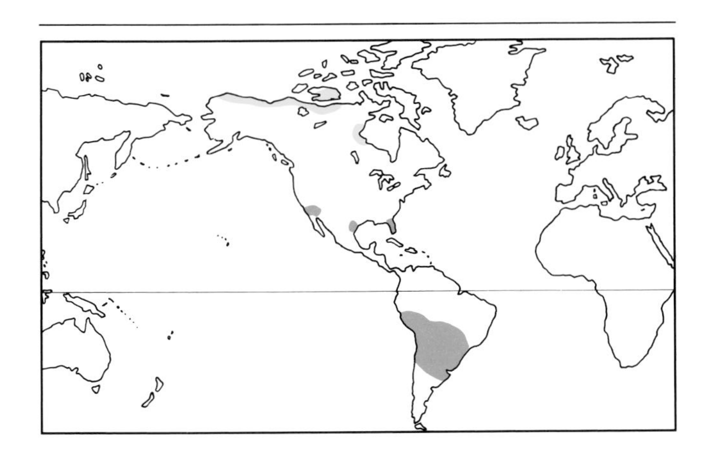

clear preference for shallow grassy pools, flooded marshes, and the shores of ponds and lakes. Less frequently on hard, sandy beaches and tidal mudflats.

Food Mainly adult and larval beetles, small molluscs and larval insects, with probably a few seeds and berries also taken.

Range Breeds in northern Alaska to north-eastern Ontario. Some winter in southern United States, Mexico, and Caribbean, but most spend non-breeding season in central South America.

Movements After nesting has taken place, birds of the year head southward from mid-August. The majority pass through central Canada and the USA, but rather more reach the Atlantic seaboard than in the spring, though occurrences on Pacific coast are rare at that time. Spring passage is largely concentrated in the North American interior, birds passing through rather quickly from mid-March.

RECORD OF SIGHTINGS	
Date ______	Date ______
Place ______	Place ______
Male(s) ______ Female(s) ______	Male(s) ______ Female(s) ______
Immature ______ Eclipse ______	Immature ______ Eclipse ______
Behavior Notes	

Bird in breeding plumage

Common Snipe

Gallinago gallinago 9½–10½ in

Nest A well-hidden scrape lined with grasses
Egg clutch 4
Egg color Olive gray, blotched with dark brown and black
Laid April–May
Incubation 18–19 days
Fledging Around 15 days

Identification Usually seen as a silhouette when it explodes from cover, flying off in an erratic zigzag manner. If observed on the ground, the plumage is seen to be a mixture of rich browns, blacks, and yellows. The upperparts are heavily mottled and barred the colors producing the effect of longitudinal stripes. The crown is black, with a central buff streak above and below the eye. The eye is set high up in the head, thus allowing the bird all-round vision as it probes for food with the full length of its long, straight bill. The legs and feet are pale green, and the bill is brown. The sexes are similar.
Voice A harsh "scaap" note uttered as it flies when startled.
Habitat From lowland marshy ground to more elevated boggy moorland. Sometimes in much drier locations.
Food Worms and a wide variety of invertebrates, insects and their larvae; at times seeds are eaten.

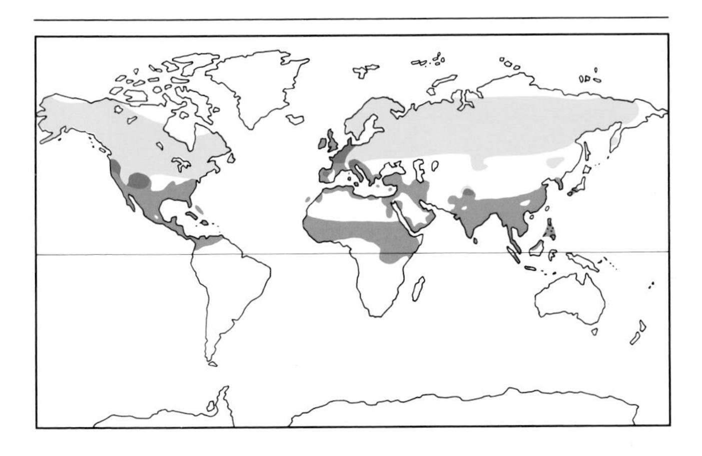

Range There are three races of Common Snipe, two of which occur in the western Palearctic. The North American race *delicata* is the more distinct of the three, having eight pairs of tail feathers (as opposed to seven on the nominate race), while the axillaries show wider brown bars. The white trailing edge of the wing is also marginally narrower than in *gallinago*. Breeds from sub-arctic Canada southward, though only very locally in California, Arizona, and Colorado, east to New Jersey. Winters in southerly parts of the breeding range south to Columbia and Venezuela.

Movements After breeding, birds move southward from July-August onward, with return passage March-April through to May.

<table>
<tr><th colspan="2">RECORD OF SIGHTINGS</th></tr>
<tr><td>Date ____________
Place ____________
Male(s) ______ Female(s) ______
Immature ____ Eclipse ______</td><td>Date ____________
Place ____________
Male(s) ______ Female(s) ______
Immature ____ Eclipse ______</td></tr>
<tr><td colspan="2">Behavior Notes</td></tr>
</table>

American Woodcock

Scolopax minor 10–11½ in

Nest A shallow depression on forest floor
Egg clutch 4
Egg color Buff, sparingly spotted with brown and gray
Laid January–April, depending on latitude
Incubation 19–21 days
Fledging 14–21 days

Identification Like its European counterpart, this bird is also largely nocturnal and is usually only seen on its dawn to dusk display, or when unexpectedly flushed from thick cover. The general plumage pattern is rusty brown above, intricately barred and mottled with black and gray. There are broad black transverse bars on the crown, and the large eyes are placed high up and well back on the head. The tail feathers are black on the underside, with prominent shining white tips particularly conspicuous during the bird's display. When flushed from cover during the daytime it jumps up and then flies off, twisting and turning through the trees. There are two clear gray Vs on the edge of the mantle and scapulars, while the underparts and underwings show a uniform rusty-buff color, lacking any trace of black barring — clear differences from the Eurasian Woodcock.
Voice A whistling or twittering call, uttered in flight.

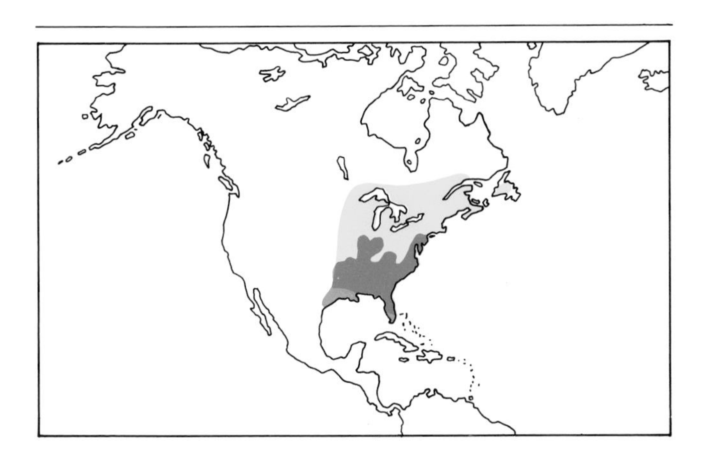

Habitat Breeds in mixed deciduous woodland with plenty of undergrowth. In winter found in more open woodland and gardens, as well as pastures, fallow fields, and pine uplands.
Food Mostly earthworms, but also beetles and fly larvae.
Range The eastern half of North America, north to southern Ontario and Quebec, New Brunswick, Nova Scotia and south-west Newfoundland. Also extends west to the eastern Dakotas, Nebraska, Kansas, and Oklahoma. A winter visitor only to southern Texas, Louisiana, and Florida. A vagrant west to Montana and Colorado; has occurred in Bermuda.
Movements Migratory in its northern range, moving south for the winter during October.

RECORD OF SIGHTINGS	
Date ______	Date ______
Place ______	Place ______
Male(s) ____ Female(s) ____	Male(s) ____ Female(s) ____
Immature ____ Eclipse ____	Immature ____ Eclipse ____
Behavior Notes	

Ruddy Turnstone

Arenaria interpres 8–10 in

Nest A shallow cup on well-vegetated rocky or gravelly ground
Egg clutch 4
Egg color Glossy brownish or olive green, with some gray mottling and black spots
Laid June
Incubation 24 days
Fledging 24–26 days

Identification In summer plumage both sexes have a pied head and upper breast, forming a strong facial pattern and black chest band. The male has a whiter crown at this stage. The mantle and wings are predominantly chestnut with bands of black. The lower breast and belly are pure white. In flight shows a white stripe down the center of the back and a pair of white shoulder stripes. There is a white wing bar, a white tail with a black subterminal band, giving the bird an unmistakable pattern. The legs are orange-red and the short beak is black. In winter the head, back, and coverts are brown, but the basic design of the plumage is essentially the same. At all times the distinctive feeding behavior of flicking over shoreline debris and turning shells and stones over to get at food give the bird its name. Juveniles are dark brown above, with a white throat, dark breast band and white below; legs are orange-red.
Voice A rapid staccato "trik-tuc-tuc-tuc" call.
Habitat In breeding seasons favors rocky coastal islands to more elevated Arctic tundra. In winter prefers seaweed-covered rocks, pebbly beaches and, to a lesser extent, muddy and sandy areas.

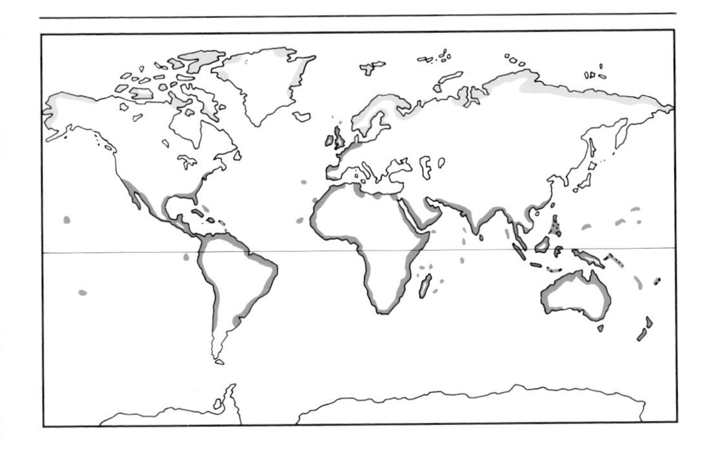

Food On the breeding grounds eats mainly plant material, but also larval insects and other invertebrates; at other times sandhoppers, molluscs, crustaceans, and fly larvae.
Range Breeding area spans the Arctic from Alaska to Siberia, penetrating as far south as Sweden. In the winter can be found around the coasts of all the warm continents. A substantial number remain on the Atlantic fringe of western Europe.
Movements A hardy, long-distance traveler to be found on beaches throughout the world. In spring moves north to reach breeding grounds late May to early June, returning southward from end of July onward.

RECORD OF SIGHTINGS	
Date ______	Date ______
Place ______	Place ______
Male(s) ____ Female(s) ____	Male(s) ____ Female(s) ____
Immature ____ Eclipse ____	Immature ____ Eclipse ____
Behavior Notes	

Birds in breeding plumage

Black Turnstone

Arenaria melanocephala 8½–10 in

Nest In grass, but sometimes on bare mud, with little or no lining
Egg clutch 4
Egg color Olive, with dark brown spots and blotches of brown
Laid Mid-May
Incubation 21–22 days
Fledging 10–14 days

Identification Fractionally larger than the Ruddy Turnstone, it can be distinguished at all times from that bird by the near-uniform slate gray upperparts, dark chin, throat and breast, and its duller dark reddish-brown legs. In breeding areas there are fine white streaks on the head and breast, a whitish supercilium, and a large whitish patch at the base of the bill. When flying, shows a pattern of light and dark, which is essentially the same as the Ruddy Turnstone's: white wing bars, rump and sides to the tail, and a white patch at the base of each wing and in the center of the lower back. However, there is a little less white on the rump and its wing bar is broader. Always looks much blacker than Ruddy Turnstone, but juveniles are a little browner, with a fine pattern of buff fringes to the feathers of the upperparts.
Voice A trilling "skirr" and a guttural rattle. On breeding grounds when disturbed utters a clear piping "weet-weet too-weet."

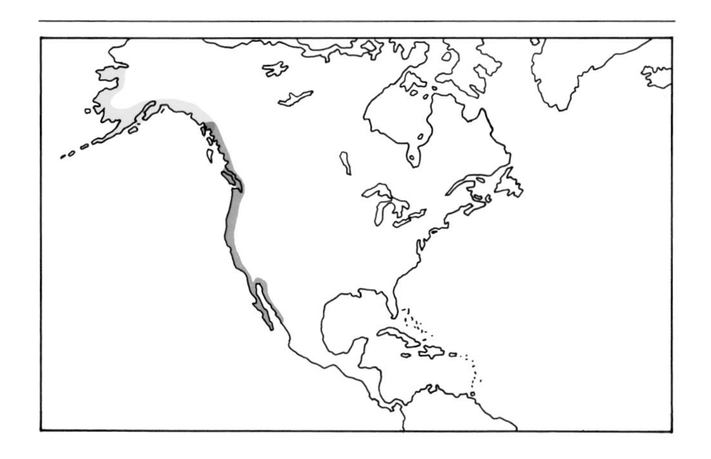

Habitat For nesting chooses grass-covered shorelines of brackish pools and tidal sloughs. During winter found on rocky coasts, jetties, barnacle-covered reefs and islets. Rarely on sandy beaches or mudflats.
Food Feeds like Ruddy Turnstone, taking similar food, such as small shrimps and molluscs.
Range Breeds on the coastal plain of western Alaska. In winter reaches as far south as the Gulf of California. A vagrant inland in the Pacific coast states and provinces.
Movements On spring passage occurs as far west as Wrangel Island in the far eastern USSR. Some immature birds remain in their winter quarters all the year.

RECORD OF SIGHTINGS	
Date ______	Date ______
Place ______	Place ______
Male(s) ______ Female(s) ______	Male(s) ______ Female(s) ______
Immature ______ Eclipse ______	Immature ______ Eclipse ______
Behavior Notes	

In winter plumage

Surfbird

Aphriza virgata 9–9½in

Nest A shallow natural depression lined with lichen and moss
Egg clutch 3–4
Egg color Buff, boldly marked with brown
Laid May
Incubation About 28 days
Fledging Probably 28–35 days

Identification In summer plumage the head, neck, and breast are white, very heavily flecked with dark gray to give a grayish impression at a distance. The rest of the underparts are white, with large and bold black chevrons along the flanks. The upper back is finely variegated in black and buff but most prominent are the scapulars, which are bright rusty-buff with black tips, forming a conspicuous patch of color on an otherwise drab bird. The bill is short with a yellow ocher base. The legs are yellowish. In winter superficially similar to a large, pale Black Turnstone. In flight shows a prominent white wing bar and a white rump. The juvenile resembles a winter-plumaged adult.

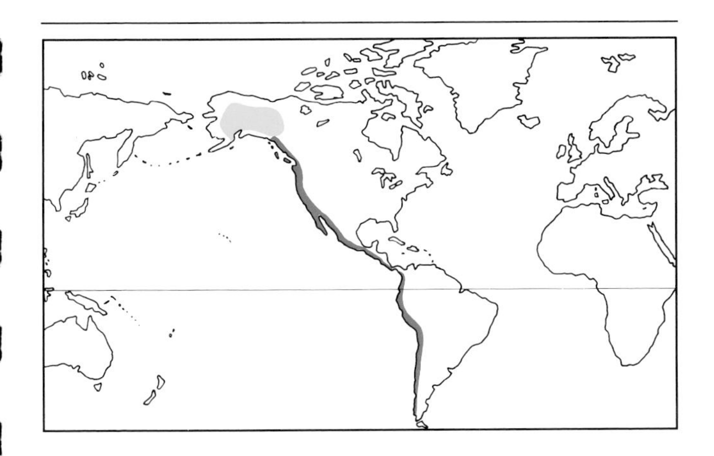

Voice Often silent but utters a whistled "kee-wee-ah" at times.
Habitat In breeding season favors the alpine zone above the tree-line; at other times, rocky coasts, sometimes sandy beaches, but rarely found on mud.
Food On breeding territory, flies and beetles. Mussels, barnacles, and periwinkles form the major part of its diet in winter quarters.
Range Breeds in Alaska and north-west Canada, wintering along the Pacific coasts of the Americas, south to Tierra del Fuego. A rare spring migrant in Texas, and vagrant to Pennsylvania.
Movements Leaves breeding ground after nesting, often as early as July, moving south along coast. Birds return in April and May.

RECORD OF SIGHTINGS	
Date ______	Date ______
Place ______	Place ______
Male(s) ____ Female(s) ____	Male(s) ____ Female(s) ____
Immature ____ Eclipse ____	Immature ____ Eclipse ____
Behavior Notes	

In winter plumage

Rock Sandpiper

Calidris ptilocnemis 8–9 in

Nest Small cup shaped in tundra vegetation
Egg clutch 4
Egg color Greenish, blotched and spotted dark brown with some blackish lines
Laid May/June
Incubation 20 days
Fledging Probably 3–4 weeks

Identification A medium-sized, stocky sandpiper with comparatively long greenish-yellow legs and a long, slightly drooping bill, which is greenish-yellow at the base. There are four races of this bird. Three of these are very like the Purple Sandpiper (fortunately the breeding or wintering ranges of the two species do not overlap). They are sooty black, with a purple sheen in winter, and more variegated with chestnut above and whitish below in the breeding season. However, they show more sharply-defined spotting on the underparts than the Purple Sandpiper in non-breeding and juvenile plumages. The fourth race (resident in the Pribilov Islands) is more distinct, and in summer plumage is vaguely similar to a Dunlin, having a black patch on the belly, not the lower breast. In winter this race is pale gray above, mottled gray and white on the breast, with a short supercilium. The bill and legs are dark. Juveniles are less distinctive. In flight there is a white wing bar (more evident in the Pribilov Islands race) and a dark tail.
Voice A "whit" or "tit" contact call.
Habitat Coastal tundra in summer and rocky shores similar to

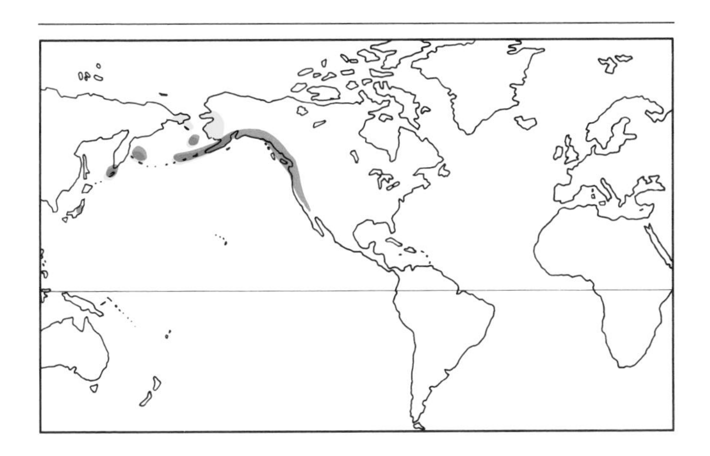

Purple Sandpiper during winter.
Food Small molluscs, crustaceans, algae, worms, and insects.
Range Resident in the Kuril and Commander Isles of the Kamchatka Peninsula of eastern Siberia, and the Pribilov Islands and the Aleutian chain off Alaska. It is a summer visitor to the Chukotskiy Peninsula of far-eastern Siberia, and the southern Alaskan mainland.
Movements Birds that breed on the Chukotskiy Peninsula and in southern Alaska are late migrants to the western coast of the USA, as far south as northern California, and also to the Tokyo area of Japan (but not the intervening areas on the coast of Siberia). Returns to breeding grounds by early April.

RECORD OF SIGHTINGS	
Date ______	Date ______
Place ______	Place ______
Male(s) ______ Female(s) ______	Male(s) ______ Female(s) ______
Immature ______ Eclipse ______	Immature ______ Eclipse ______
Behavior Notes	

In breeding plumage

Purple Sandpiper

Calidris maritima 8–9in

Nest	Small cup shaped in tundra vegetation
Egg clutch	4
Egg color	Greenish, blotched and spotted dark brown with some blackish lines
Laid	June
Incubation	21 days
Fledging	Probably 3–4 weeks

Identification At all times a dark-plumaged, portly bird with quite a long, yellow-based drooping bill and short yellow legs. In winter is dark slate-gray on the head, neck, back, and wings, and on much of the upper breast. Slim, paler fringes are evident on the coverts and tertials, while adults show a small white chin. The belly and undertail coverts are whitish, often flecked with gray at the sides. At times the upperparts have a purple hue, hence the name. In summer the basic plumage remains dark but takes on a browner tone, with the crown and scapulars becoming more scaly-looking, being edged with gold, chestnut, and white. There is a pale, indistinct supercilium. Juvenile plumage is not unlike adult's summer dress. In flight the dark tail is bordered by a bright white lateral upper tail covert, and there is a slim white wing bar.

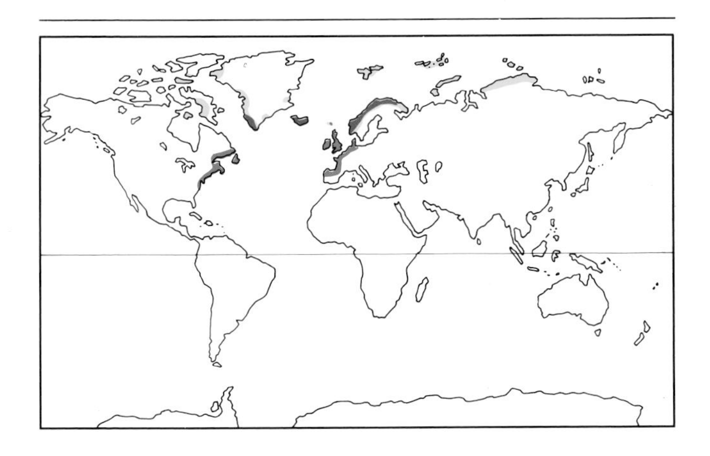

Voice A "whit" or "tit" contact call.
Habitat Breeds on the Arctic tundra. Spends the whole winter on low rocky coasts; sometimes to be found on jetties, piers, and breakwaters, and very occasionally on sandy or muddy shores.
Food Small molluscs, crustaceans, algae, worms, and insects.
Range Breeds on the Canadian islands to Siberia, as well as Iceland and upland Scandinavia. Most Canadian birds winter on the north-east coast of North America, though some are found around the Great Lakes.
Movements Does not undertake the long-distance movements typical of other sandpipers, but tends to spread out over suitable habitat, perhaps less than 1000 miles south of the breeding area.

<table>
<tr><th colspan="2">RECORD OF SIGHTINGS</th></tr>
<tr><td>Date ______
Place ______
Male(s) ______ Female(s) ______
Immature ______ Eclipse ______</td><td>Date ______
Place ______
Male(s) ______ Female(s) ______
Immature ______ Eclipse ______</td></tr>
<tr><td colspan="2">Behavior Notes</td></tr>
</table>

In winter plumage

Red Knot

Calidris canutus 9–9½in

Nest A scrape on dry rocky ground
Egg clutch 3 or 4
Egg color Glossy, pale olive green, with small brown markings
Laid June
Incubation 21 days
Fledging 20 days

Identification A stout, round, medium-sized bird with short greenish-gray legs and black bill. It is well known for its large communal gatherings and impressive aerial flights in winter quarters. A plain, medium gray above with an indistinct pale supercilium, the underparts are dull white, suffused with pale gray on the breast. In flight it shows an indistinct pale gray rump and a pencil-thin wing bar along its length. The change to summer plumage is most dramatic, as adults acquire rich orange-chestnut underparts from face to belly, while the upperparts become a mixture of black, white, chestnut, and gold.
Voice "Puk" or "knut," hence the bird's name.
HabitatThe summer home is high Arctic tundra with large open mudflats, which are backed by salt-marshes and fields in winter.

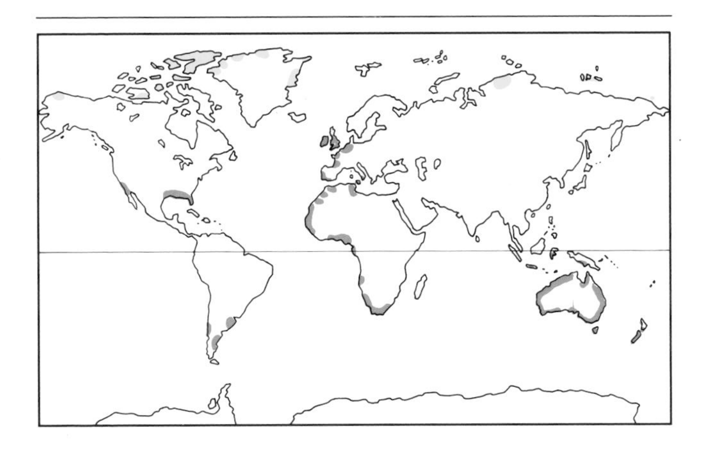

Food Mainly invertebrates, chiefly molluscs, crustaceans, worms and insects with larval insects; some plant material when on its breeding grounds.
Range Has a fragmented distribution throughout the Holarctic. The Canadian Islands, Greenland and Siberia are main nesting strongholds.
Movements Leaves breeding grounds late July or early August, dispersing in four general directions: south to South America, to western Europe, to West Africa, and some to Australia and New Zealand.

RECORD OF SIGHTINGS	
Date ______	Date ______
Place ______	Place ______
Male(s) ______ Female(s) ______	Male(s) ______ Female(s) ______
Immature ______ Eclipse ______	Immature ______ Eclipse ______
Behavior Notes	

In immature plumage

Dunlin

Calidris alpina 6½–8½ in

Nest Small depression well hidden in vegetation
Egg clutch 4
Egg color Pale greenish to olive-buff, with gray spots
Laid April, May or June, depending on latitude
Incubation 22 days
Fledging 20 days

Identification A small, dumpy, highly active bird generally considered the "yardstick" against which many other small waders can be compared. During the winter a dull gray-brown bird, the upperparts being rather plain, while the breast is lightly streaked gray, with the remainder of the underparts white. In breeding plumage its large black belly patch contrasts with white vent and flanks and darker streaked breast, while the black-centered mantle and scapular feathers show varying bright chestnut, gray and white borders. The legs are medium length and black. The bill is rather long, black, and drooped at the tip. In flight shows a conspicuous narrow white wing bar, white sides to the rump and upper tail, and a white underwing. There are six races of the Dunlin, which vary slightly from each other. The two American races *pacifica* and *hudsonia* are the largest, and also the brightest-colored on the back, hence the bird's other common name, "Red-backed Sandpiper."
Voice A shrill "treep" or "kree" call.
Habitat Nests in a variety of situations, from peat moorland to salt-marsh in the south, to Arctic tussock tundra in the north. In winter prefers extensive areas of tidal mudflats, or anywhere with mud-fringed water.
Food Inter-tidal invertebrates, including rag worms, bivalves, small

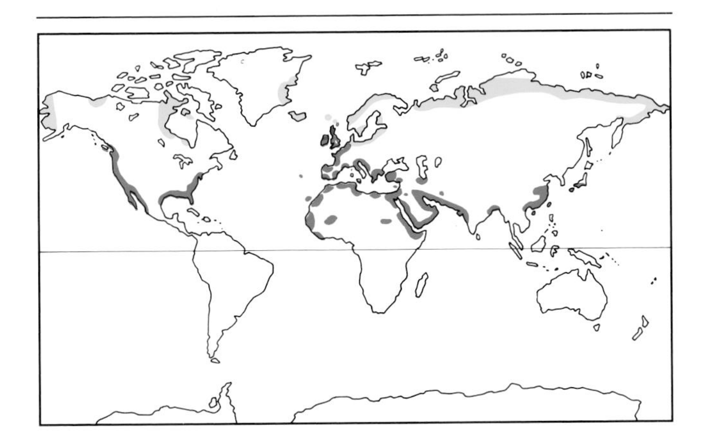

molluscs, and planktonic crustacea during the winter. On breeding grounds adult and larval insects, beetles, spiders, mites, earthworms, and sometimes seeds.

Range Circumpolar in its breeding distribution, the race *pacifica* breeds in western Alaska, and winters along the west coast of USA and Mexico. The race *hudsonia* breeds in central Canada and winters in south-eastern USA.

Movements In spring general move north begins March or April. Birds take a west coast route and may cut across the Gulf of Alaska. Others move up from the south-east via Hudson Bay. Return passage begins late July or August, and lasts through September and October, or even into November.

RECORD OF SIGHTINGS	
Date ______	Date ______
Place ______	Place ______
Male(s) ____ Female(s) ____	Male(s) ____ Female(s) ____
Immature ____ Eclipse ____	Immature ____ Eclipse ____
Behavior Notes	

In breeding plumage

Sanderling

Calidris alba 8–8½in

Nest	Scrape lined with small leaves or other vegetation
Egg clutch	4
Egg color	Greenish-olive, sometimes brownish, with sparse darker spotting
Laid	June
Incubation	28 days
Fledging	17 days

Identification About the same size as a Dunlin, it is rather more thickset with black legs and a short, straight, black bill. One of the palest-looking waders during winter, with brilliant white underparts, a bright silver back and a prominent black patch on the inner wing at the shoulder. The dark eye shows up well on the birds's almost white head. Summer plumage comprises a bright chestnut coloring on the head, upper breast and upperparts. The lower breast and belly remain bright white, while on the mantle and scapulars, gray and white flecking is mixed in with the chestnut coloring. Flight is fast and sometimes erratic, showing a broad white bar along the wing.
Voice A distinctive "twick."
Habitat Flat tundra with some vegetation, usually near water, during breeding season. At other times prefers long, sandy beaches.

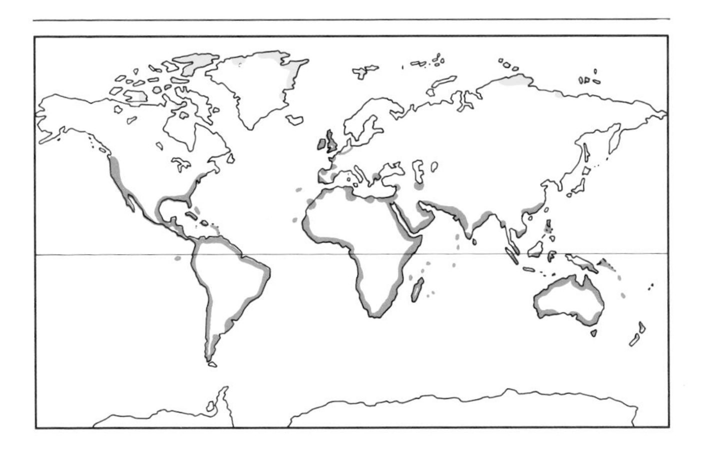

Food Adult and larval dipteran flies, small beetles, sandhoppers, spiders and burrowing amphipods. On breeding ground plant buds, seeds, algae, and mosses are also taken.
Range Breeds in three major areas: Arctic Canada, Greenland, and Siberia. To be found on virtually any suitable beach throughout the world when not nesting.
Movements Birds leave their breeding grounds in late July to mid-August, occurring on both east and west coasts during the fall passage period. In spring movement back to nesting territories begins March and April through to May, when again to be found on both seaboards.

RECORD OF SIGHTINGS	
Date ______	Date ______
Place ______	Place ______
Male(s) ______ Female(s) ______	Male(s) ______ Female(s) ______
Immature ______ Eclipse ______	Immature ______ Eclipse ______
Behavior Notes	

In winter plumage

Semipalmated Sandpiper

Calidris pusilla 5–6in

Nest Depression in ground, or hummock or knoll
Egg clutch 4
Egg color Dull white to olive-buff, with reddish-brown speckles
Laid June
Incubation 19–20 days
Fledging 16 days

Identification In summer plumage a rather dull-looking bird, with the upperparts a mixture of black, buff, and gray. The underparts are white, while there is an extensive streaked breast band. The dark bill is short and straight with a deep base. It is blunt-tipped in profile and in good head-on views usually shows a slight expansion of the tip. The legs are blackish. In flight a narrow whitish wing bar and white sides to rump and tail can be seen. In winter plumage there is no extensive streaking on the breast or darker marking on the upperparts.
Voice A harsh, low-pitched "churk" or "chrup." Sometimes utters a "chirrup" reminiscent of a Pectoral Sandpiper. On breeding ground has a monotonous trilling "pee pee see" or "di-jip di-jip" uttered in a trilling aerial display.
Habitat Wet coastal and low inland tundra for nesting. Winters in large flocks on estuary mudflats.
Food Insects and inter-tidal invertebrates.
Range Breeds from mouth of the River Yukon on the west coast of Alaska east to Victoria Island, around Hudson Bay on to Baffin

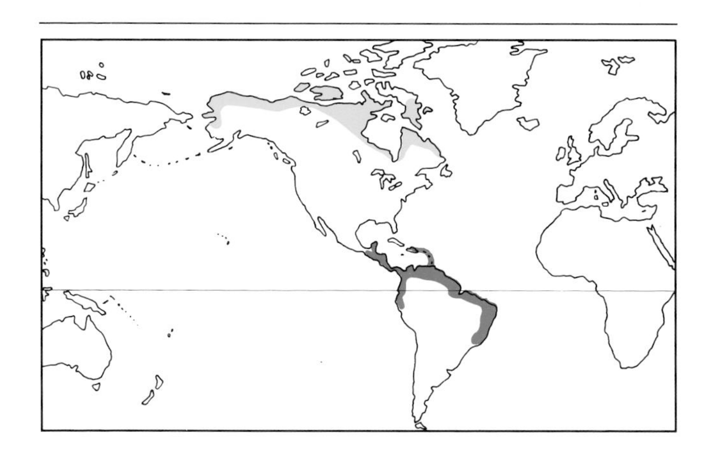

Island and Labrador. Winters on Pacific coast of Central America, north to Guatemala, in the West Indies, and in coastal South America to Peru and Uruguay.

Movements Birds from different breeding areas take different migratory routes south across North America: Alaskan birds pass through the Great Plains; the central Canadian population moves south-east; eastern birds move via the Gulf of St Lawrence across the Atlantic direct to the Caribbean. In spring the central Canadian population joins Alaskan birds on migration through the Great Plains, while east Canadian birds follow the Atlantic coast northwards.

RECORD OF SIGHTINGS	
Date ______	Date ______
Place ______	Place ______
Male(s) ______ Female(s) ______	Male(s) ______ Female(s) ______
Immature ______ Eclipse ______	Immature ______ Eclipse ______
Behavior Notes	

In breeding plumage

Western Sandpiper

Calidris mauri 5½–6½in

Nest Well hidden under a small bush
Egg clutch 4
Egg color Creamy, spotted and blotched dark brown
Laid June
Incubation 21 days
Fledging 19 days

Identification Often difficult to distinguish from Semipalmated Sandpiper, but in breeding plumage points of difference are rusty-orange centers to upper scapulars, and rufous patch on crown and ear coverts, contrasting with gray wing coverts, nape, and mantle. The breast is heavily marked, with dark streaks often extending as a distinctive line of chevrons along the flanks. The black bill, of variable length, usually has a slightly decurved drooped tip. The legs are also black. In winter plumage almost identical to Semipalmated Sandpiper. However, juvenile Western Sandpipers are relatively distinct, being less scaly and less uniform, also paler faced with less defined supercilium and dark eye stripe.
Voice On the breeding ground the song is a series of ascending notes followed by a buzzing trill. The typical call is a thin squeaky "jeet" or "cheep."
Habitat Well-drained tundra from sea level to the lower slopes of the mountains, preferring ridges and hummocks of heath interspersed with low-lying small pools and lakes for nesting. During winter haunts open mudflats.

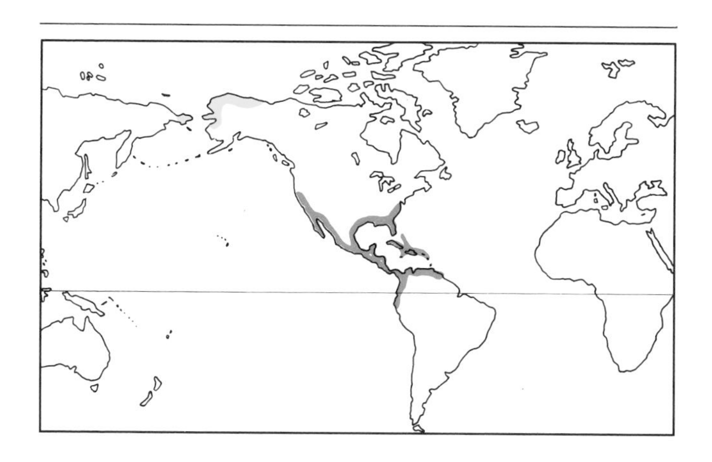

Food Mostly insects, especially flies.
Range As a breeding bird confined to northern and western Alaska and the east coast of the Chukotskiy Peninsula in extreme eastern Siberia. In winter found along the Pacific coast from California south to Peru, on the Gulf of Mexico, on the Atlantic coast north to New England, in the Caribbean, and on the Atlantic coast of South America east to Surinam.
Movements After breeding, the whole population moves south through the Pacific states and provinces. Most follow the coast, but some move inland on coastal states. Small numbers move south-east to the Atlantic coast, from Massachusetts southward.

RECORD OF SIGHTINGS	
Date ______	Date ______
Place ______	Place ______
Male(s) ______ Female(s) ______	Male(s) ______ Female(s) ______
Immature ______ Eclipse ______	Immature ______ Eclipse ______
Behavior Notes	

In winter plumage

Least Sandpiper

Calidris minutilla 5–6in

Nest Shallow depression lined with dry leaves or grass
Egg clutch 4
Egg color Pale buff, spotted and blotched with brown
Laid June
Incubation 19–23 days
Fledging 21 days or thereabouts

Identification Marginally the smallest shorebird in the world. In breeding plumage looks dark brown at a distance, with dingy well-streaked head and breast. Closer inspection reveals a fine, pale V at the side of the mantle, and a rusty tone to the crown and ear coverts and upperparts. The underparts are white. The bill is short and fine, curving gradually throughout its full length. Legs are pale yellowish, greenish, or brownish. Winter plumage looks dark brownish-gray with the dark centers of the feathers on the upperparts producing a slightly blotchy effect. There is a neat dusky breast and quite a prominent pale supercilium. The juvenile looks quite bright and may recall the Little Stint or a tiny Pectoral Sandpiper in its general plumage pattern. In flight shows a white wing bar and white sides to the rump.
Voice A shrill, high, rolling "kreeep" or disyllabic "kre-ep," as well as a lower-pitched, vibrant "prrrt."
Habitat Marshy areas within spruce forests, sedge meadows, flat sandy islands and boggy tundra for nesting. Less coastal in winter, occurring in upper reaches of salt-marshes, as well as inland on the margins of fresh water and in wet grazing meadows.

Food Small insects, flies, larvae, and tiny marine invertebrates.
Range Breeds in western Alaska through northern Canada, south to north-west British Columbia, northern Ontario, and Nova Scotia, and east to Southampton Island and northern Labrador. Winters in Gulf of Mexico, Caribbean, and west South America.
Movements Spring passage quite late, peaking in the first three weeks of May. Birds move over the Caribbean to the Gulf of Mexico and Florida, flying up the Atlantic coast to reach breeding grounds in early June. After breeding, they leave breeding grounds from mid-July onward, peak numbers occurring in August and September.

RECORD OF SIGHTINGS	
Date ______	Date ______
Place ______	Place ______
Male(s) ______ Female(s) ______	Male(s) ______ Female(s) ______
Immature ______ Eclipse ______	Immature ______ Eclipse ______
Behavior Notes	

Moulting into breeding plumage

White-rumped Sandpiper

Calidris fusicollis 6–7in

Nest A deep depression in soil or grass lined with grass and dead leaves
Egg clutch 4
Egg color Greenish to olive-buff, blotched and spotted with brown
Laid June
Incubation 21–22 days
Fledging 16–17 days

Identification In breeding plumage is mottled with buff, gray, and black on the upperparts, with a rusty tinge to the crown, ear coverts, and scapulars. The throat and breast are streaked and spotted with black, the streaks becoming larger black Vs on the flanks. The underparts are white. The short, straight bill is blackish, often with a dull green or yellowish base. The legs are black. In flight shows a narrow white wing bar. The white "rump" is, in fact, a white band on the upper tail. In winter is dun-gray above, when it shows a prominent white supercilium. The breast is washed gray with finer dark markings. The juvenile is scaly above and has prominent splashes of chestnut on the fringes of the back and crown feathers. There is a white "brace" on the sides of the mantle and a contrastingly gray hind-neck and breast. The latter is well streaked, and a few of the streaks extend to the flanks. A white supercilium sets off a chestnut cap.
Voice A strange, quiet high-pitched squeak, a "jeet."
Habitat Wet lowland and upland tundra is the usual nesting requirement. In winter frequents lake shores, wet pastures, and sea beaches, brackish swamps and especially mudflats, where it can be found in large numbers.
Food Tiny molluscs, insects, small worms, and seeds.
Range Arctic Canada from northern Mackenzie to southern Baffin

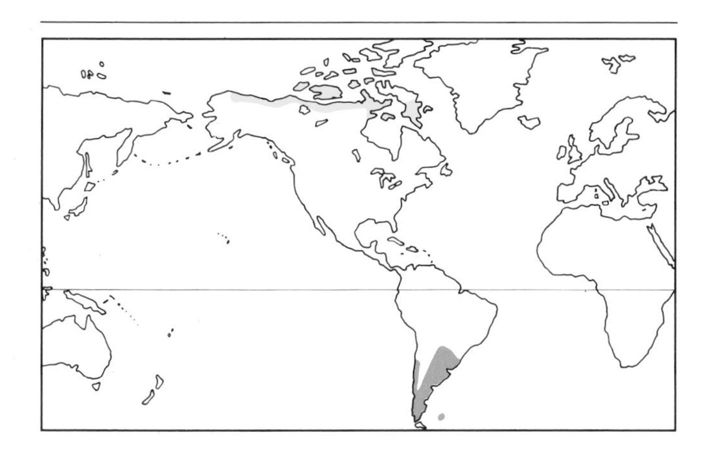

Island, occasionally northern Alaska. Winters South America, mainly east of the Andes and south of the Equator, mostly from southern Brazil to Tierra del Fuego and Falkland Islands. Spring passage northwards is more westerly than in the fall, overflying the Great Antilles and Gulf of Mexico, and across the Great Plains.
Movements Birds arrive at their breeding haunts in May or early June. Rare on Atlantic coast in spring, and infrequent visitor to the interior Pacific states. Peak passage in April – May. Departure from breeding grounds is leisurely. Males leave early July but juveniles do not reach USA until late September. Most move through interior North America, then along the Atlantic flyway and across the west Atlantic to northern South America.

RECORD OF SIGHTINGS	
Date ______	Date ______
Place ______	Place ______
Male(s) ______ Female(s) ______	Male(s) ______ Female(s) ______
Immature ______ Eclipse ______	Immature ______ Eclipse ______
Behavior Notes	

In winter plumage

Baird's Sandpiper

Calidris bairdii 5½–6½in

Nest Exposed scrape in short vegetation
Egg clutch 4
Egg color Buff-colored, thickly spotted with brown
Laid June
Incubation 19–21 days
Fledging 20 days

Identification Generally buffer-looking than White-rumped Sandpiper, it lacks the brighter tones of that species in breeding and juvenile plumage. However, always shows a neat, finely-streaked breast band and unstreaked flanks. There is a less well-marked supercilium than White-rumped Sandpiper. At all times the fine-tipped bill and legs are blackish. In summer adults are quite "mealy" in appearance above, their plumage consisting of a mixture of buff, black, and gray, with large black centers to the central scapulars. In winter they are gray-brown above, with fine, pale scaling only obvious at close quarters. The juvenile is dull gray-brown, with neat buff or whitish fringes to the upperparts, giving it a distinctive scaly appearance. The underparts are white in all plumages. In flight shows a narrow white wing bar and narrow white sides to tail.
Voice A low, raspy, trilling "preeet" or "kreeep."
Habitat Favored breeding situation is dry, elevated tundra. At other times, freshwater margins, damp fields, as well as dry areas of short cropland and pasture.
Food All manner of small invertebrates, plus insects and spiders.
Range The high Arctic from Chukotskiy Peninsula in north-east Siberia, across northern Alaska and Canada, east to Baffin Island and north-west Greenland. Wintering area is South America.

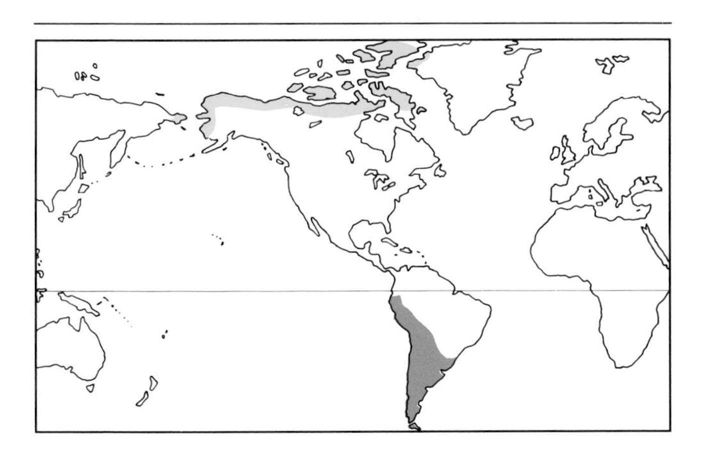

Movements Has unusual migration route that is well inland and concentrated along the backbone of the continents – the Rockies and the Andes. Birds begin to leave winter quarters early March, undertaking long-distance flights, passing over Central America without stopping and moving northwards through the interior of North America in April and May. After breeding, adults leave Arctic in late July, moving south through Canada to west of Hudson Bay and on to the prairies of northern USA. Here they feed up for a non-stop flight of some 4000 miles via a great circle over the eastern Pacific to the Andes. Most adults have left the USA by mid-August, taking about five weeks to complete the journey. Juveniles migrate at a more leisurely pace.

RECORD OF SIGHTINGS	
Date ______	Date ______
Place ______	Place ______
Male(s) ____ Female(s) ____	Male(s) ____ Female(s) ____
Immature ____ Eclipse ____	Immature ____ Eclipse ____
Behavior Notes	

Adult moulting into winter plumage

Pectoral Sandpiper

Calidris melanotus 7½–9in

Nest	On ground and well hidden, made of grass, leaves and lichen
Egg clutch	4
Egg color	Greenish to buff, heavily blotched with brown
Laid	June
Incubation	21–23 days
Fledging	21 days

Identification A medium-sized sandpiper, the males are significantly larger than the females. At all times, marked by a neat, well-streaked breast or pectoral band, which is characteristically cut off from the white underparts. The bill is medium length and slightly down-curved, the basal third being olive-colored. The legs are olive to yellow. In breeding plumage adults show a mixture of black, gray and buff upperparts, with black scapulars neatly fringed with buff. There is a white V at the side of the mantle. In winter plumage the feather centers are duller with dingier, ill-defined fringes. Juveniles are similar to summer adults but have rather darker feather centers and better defined white, russet, and buff fringes, giving a neater, crisp effect. There are usually two prominent white Vs on the side of the mantle and scapulars. In flight there is a narrow white wing bar, while the black center to the rump and tail shows a prominent white area at the sides.
Voice On breeding ground a hooting "oo-af" call, at other times a harsh, reedy "churck" or "prrp."

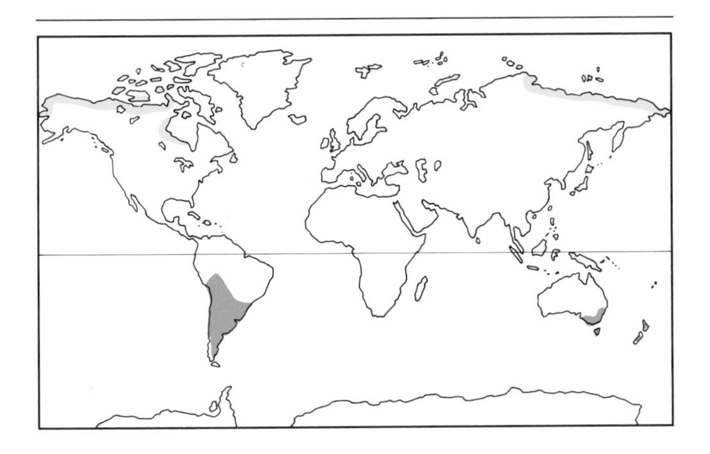

Habitat Wet flat tundra, both on coast and in foothills.
Food Insects, worms, flies, insect larvae, and sometimes crickets, grasshoppers and fiddler-crabs; occasionally, some vegetable matter.
Range Breeds in eastern Siberia to Hudson Bay. Almost the entire population winters in South America. Small numbers winter regularly in Australia and New Zealand.
Movements From March to early June birds move northward through North America, mostly in the interior and to the west of Hudson Bay, but not on the west coast. Return passage spans the period late July to September, when most of the population follows a route south-eastward over North America via south-east Canada and the Gulf of St Lawrence out over the Atlantic in a great circle to South America. Uncommon in the west during the fall.

RECORD OF SIGHTINGS	
Date ______	Date ______
Place ______	Place ______
Male(s) ____ Female(s) ____	Male(s) ____ Female(s) ____
Immature ____ Eclipse ____	Immature ____ Eclipse ____
Behavior Notes	

Upland Sandpiper

Batramia longicauda 11–13 in

Nest Well hidden in a clump of grass
Egg clutch 4
Egg color Creamy or pinkish-buff, speckled or spotted with reddish-brown
Laid June
Incubation 24 days
Fledging 33 days

Identification About the size of a Yellowlegs, its long tail projects beyond the wingtips when at rest, while a small head is supported by a neck which, when stretched, can look ridiculously thin. The short, straight bill has a darker ridge and tip. In general appearance recalls a small curlew. Notably the crown is blackish with an indistinct buffish crown stripe. Otherwise the face is plain, but the eye is prominent and staring. In flight has a cross-like outline with long wings and tail. The center of the back, rump and tail are particularly dark, as is the outer wing. From below, the heavily barred underwing and axillaries are notable. Often flies with shallow fluttering wingbeats.
Voice The flight call is a liquid, fluty "quip-quip-ip" reminiscent of a quail; on nesting grounds a bubbling "quip-ip-ip-ip-ip-ip-ip."
Habitat For nesting favors a variety of grassland settings, including prairies, hayfields, pastures and, more rarely, cultivated fields. Further north is found in clearings in spruce forests. On passage and in winter, seen in a variety of short grass habitats.
Food Insects, mainly grasshoppers, crickets and weevils, also seeds.

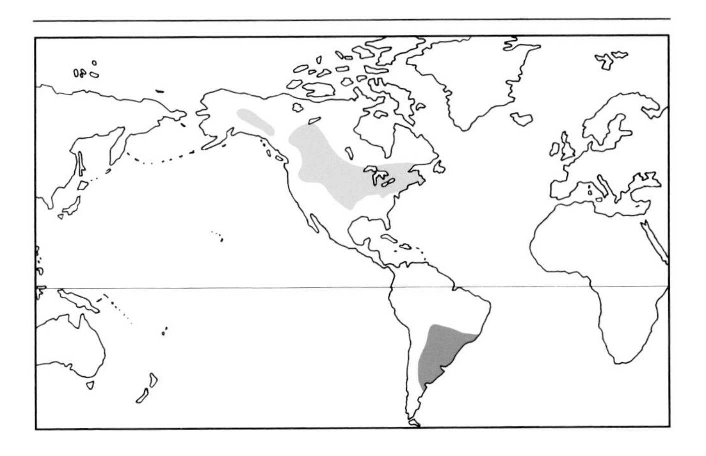

Range Breeds in interior North America from north-west Alaska south and east across western Canada and the central and eastern USA to Virginia and Maryland. Winters on the pampas of southern Brazil and Argentina, and beyond to the Rio Negro.
Movements Spring migrants reach southern USA in early March, reaching nesting areas through April to June in the northernmost parts of its range. In the fall juveniles begin to move south down the Mississippi and central flyways. By October most have left the USA, moving through eastern central America or across the Gulf of Mexico to Columbia and Venezuela. The Ontario and New England populations move south across the interior of the eastern states and over the Greater Antilles and may be found in Surinam and Brazil. It is a vagrant to the west coast.

RECORD OF SIGHTINGS	
Date ______	Date ______
Place ______	Place ______
Male(s) ______ Female(s) ______	Male(s) ______ Female(s) ______
Immature ______ Eclipse ______	Immature ______ Eclipse ______
Behavior Notes	

Buff-breasted Sandpiper

Tryngites subruficollis 7–8 in

Nest A shallow scrape
Egg clutch 4
Egg color Buff-colored, spotted with brown
Laid June
Incubation Around 28 days
Fledging Probably 3–4 weeks

Identification Adult birds have a fairly bright apricot/buff-colored face, and underparts that are unmarked apart from a few darker spots at the sides of the breast. The crown is flecked darker, giving a capped effect at times, while the remainder of the upperparts is gray or black with buff fringes. The bill is generally dark and the legs a fairly bright yellow ocher color. The small black eye surrounded by a paler orbital ring stands out in an otherwise plain-looking face that gives the bird a rather docile expression. The male birds are up to 10 percent larger than females. In flight appears fairly long-winged, which is noticeably white underneath. Juveniles are like adults but have paler broad fringes to the feathers, looking more scaly on the upperparts.
Voice A "prreet" alarm call.
Habitat Breeds on the drier slopes of grass or lichen tundra. At other times haunts dry, open grassland, and on migration will visit golf courses, airfields, and stubble fields.
Food Terrestrial insects and invertebrates, especially beetle and fly larvae.

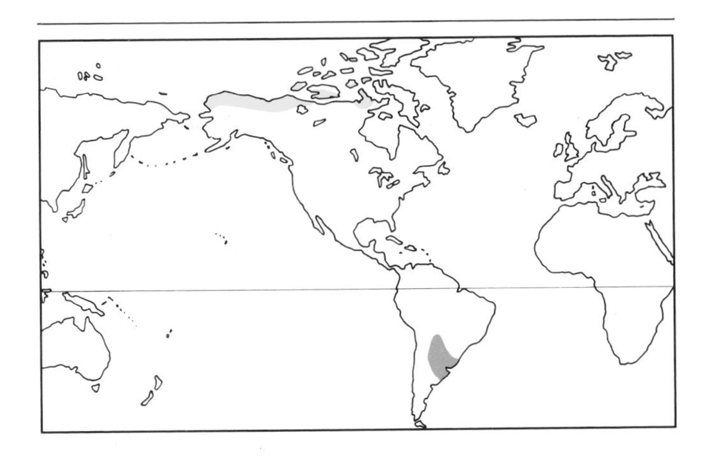

Range Breeds in northern Alaska to western Canada, with a few pairs in eastern Siberia. Winters on the Argentinian and Paraguayan pampas.

Movements Birds migrate northward through the southern United States from mid-March to May, stopping off at traditional places in Texas and later Alberta *en route* to breeding grounds. The main passage southward is through the prairies and central USA during August and September, before crossing the Gulf of Mexico to South American winter quarters in the months of September and October. A small element of the passage, mainly juveniles, heads further south and eastward, cutting across the Great Lakes and through New England, before making the long sea crossing to north-eastern South America.

RECORD OF SIGHTINGS	
Date ______	Date ______
Place ______	Place ______
Male(s) ____ Female(s) ____	Male(s) ____ Female(s) ____
Immature ____ Eclipse ____	Immature ____ Eclipse ____
Behavior Notes	

RARE MIGRANTS
AND
VAGRANTS

Ringed Plover

Charadrius hiaticula 7–8 in

Identification A small, rotund, lively shorebird, it has a prominent black collar, broad at the front and narrow behind (which is incomplete in the juvenile), a brown back and crown, with a black face and forehead. The legs are orange-yellow (flesh-colored in juveniles) and the bill is orange with a black tip. Normal flight is rapid and generally low down, when a conspicuous white wing bar is evident.

Voice A liquid "pee-u." Also has a piping "kluup" call. The song is a trilling "tooli-tooli-tooli," to be heard regularly from March to July.

Habitat In the breeding season prefers sandy and shingly seashore. Also nests on fallow land, dried mud of drained marshes near the coast, sandy headland well away from the sea, inland rivers, lakes,

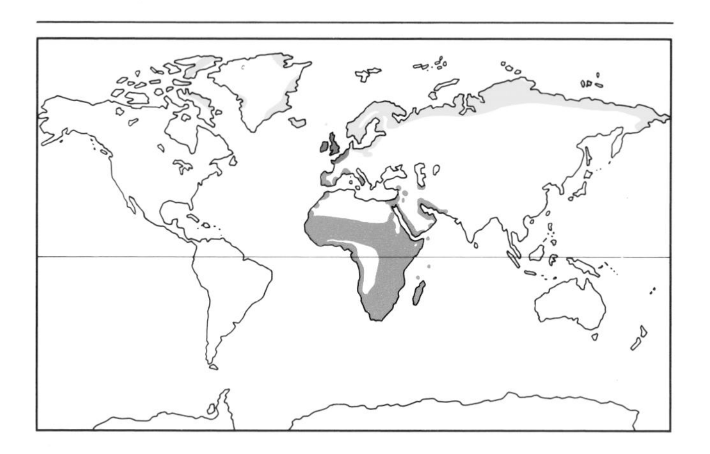

and occasionally inland reservoir margins and gravel pits. Winters on muddy and sandy estuaries. Frequently noted at inland water on passage.

Food Secures molluscs, worms or insects in typical plover fashion, taking one or two steps forward, or running to pick up whatever its keen sight has detected.

Range Breeds in Greenland, east Baffin Island, Iceland, and parts of western Europe north to Scandinavia. This bird is virtually unknown in USA, although one did breed in Alaska in 1970. The very similar Semipalmated Plover is the counterpart of this old world species.

RECORD OF SIGHTINGS	
Date ______	Date ______
Place ______	Place ______
Male(s) ______ Female(s) ______	Male(s) ______ Female(s) ______
Immature ______ Eclipse ______	Immature ______ Eclipse ______
Behavior Notes	

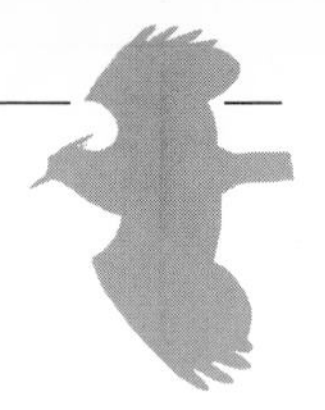

Lapwing

Vanellus vanellus 11–12½ in

Identification At a distance looks very black and white, while close observation will reveal the dark upperparts are metallic green, and the undertail coverts a rufous buff (particularly obvious when the bird comes in to land). The legs are reddish. At rest the long crest is very noticeable, and this is even more apparent in the male. In flight the slow beats of the broad, rounded wings give a distinctive flickering black and white appearance, as the birds lazily trail across the sky in straggling lines. Young birds have short crests and pale edgings to the feathers, giving the upperparts a scaly look.
Voice A shrill, often wheezy-sounding "pee-wit." When displaying, it has a longer drawn-out "pee-weet-a-weet-weet" call, most frequently uttered during its tumbling, erratic, nuptial flights in March, April and May.
Habitat Nests year-round on arable land, newly ploughed fields, moorland, rough ground, reservoir margins, sand and gravel workings. Less often found on mudflats and in other tidal situations.
Food Insects, worms, molluscs, crustacea, and vegetable matter.

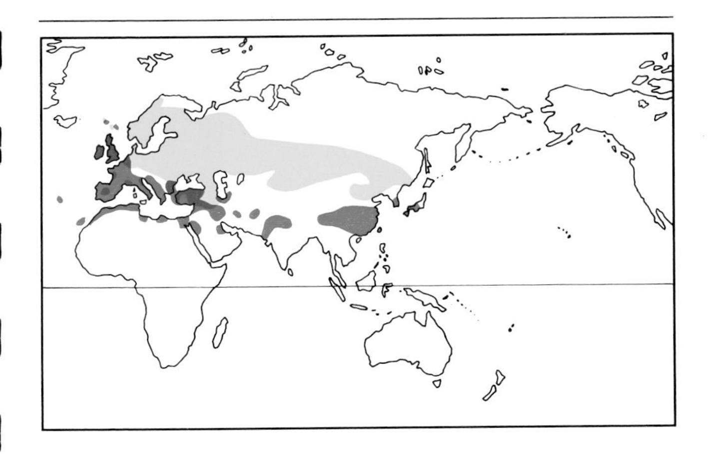

Range Breeds in Britain, Scandinavia, and eastward across Europe to Asia.

Movements Not usually known for its long migrations, many do, however, move in the winter to escape bad weather. Generally hard-weather flights tend to be in a westerly direction, when many reach Ireland. On rare occasions crosses the Atlantic to the Americas. The most notable record was in December 1927, when birds moving westward out of England were caught up in strong easterly winds sweeping them past Ireland, and several hundred ultimately reached Newfoundland. There have been other scattered occurrences of this bird reaching the eastern seaboard of North America, some as far south as the Carolinas, and West Indies.

RECORD OF SIGHTINGS	
Date ______	Date ______
Place ______	Place ______
Male(s) ____ Female(s) ____	Male(s) ____ Female(s) ____
Immature ____ Eclipse ____	Immature ____ Eclipse ____
Behavior Notes	

Black-tailed Godwit

Limosa limosa 14½–17½ in

Identification A long-billed, long-legged, graceful shorebird, the male in summer has a chestnut-colored head and breast, while the belly and flanks are white with distinct black bars. The female, though similarly colored, is duller-looking. In winter both sexes are basically gray and white, but the flight pattern is always distinctive, with its strong white wing bar, white tail with broad black terminal band of black and trailing legs identifying it immediately. Juveniles have a warm pink or buff tinge to the upperparts and breast, reminiscent of a pale adult in breeding dress. Frequently wades up to its belly to feed, at other times probes the soft sand or mud. Generally, only found in small groups, but flocks several hundred strong can occur in favored localities.
Voice A clear "wicka-wicka-wicka" uttered by birds in flight.
Habitat Nests among damp vegetation, but at other times occurs around muddy margins of fresh water in flooded fields and in favored estuaries or river valleys in winter.
Food Worms, molluscs, and crustaceans.
Range There are three separate races. The European and western Asiatic race breeds in an area stretching from Britain across to central Russia, wintering mainly in Africa and India. The Icelandic race breeds in Iceland and winters in western Europe, especially

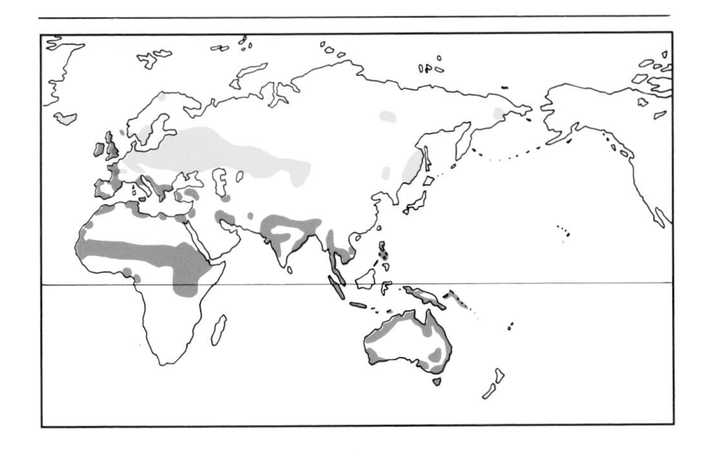

Britain and Ireland. A third race breeds in eastern Asia and winters south to Australia. The western European population is centered on the Low Countries and West Germany. In Britain the species became extinct about 150 years ago, but began to recolonize the Ouse Washes in East Anglia in the 1950s. Since then it has established a firm foothold there and has spread to new areas, though with no more than 80 pairs at a dozen widely scattered sites, it remains scarce and local. The British migrant population has also increased.

Movements The east Asian race passes through the Aleutians in spring and has occurred as a vagrant on the eastern seaboard of the USA.

RECORD OF SIGHTINGS	
Date ______________	Date ______________
Place ______________	Place ______________
Male(s) ______ Female(s) ______	Male(s) ______ Female(s) ______
Immature ______ Eclipse ______	Immature ______ Eclipse ______
Behavior Notes	

In winter plumage

Bar-tailed Godwit

Limosa lapponica 14½–16½ in

Identification In winter plumage confusion with the Black-tailed Godwit is possible, but the slightly browner and more heavily streaked upperparts and dull white underparts, as well as the shorter all-dark legs, long, slightly uptilted bill and more dumpy appearance are useful differences. In breeding dress the head, neck and underparts are a deep rufous-cinnamon or chestnut color, with the darker central mantle and scapulars showing orangy-buff edgings, but the wing coverts stay a duller gray-brown. The female remains duller-looking, only developing a warm buff-wash down the throat and breast. In flight the rather uniform brown wings, barred tail and contrasting white rump and lower back are further aids to its identification.
Voice A sharp "kak-kak" or "kirrick."
Habitat Low-lying swamp tundra for breeding; mudflats and tidal estuaries in winter.
Food Annelid worms, crustaceans, molluscs, insects, caterpillars, also berries and seeds on nesting grounds.

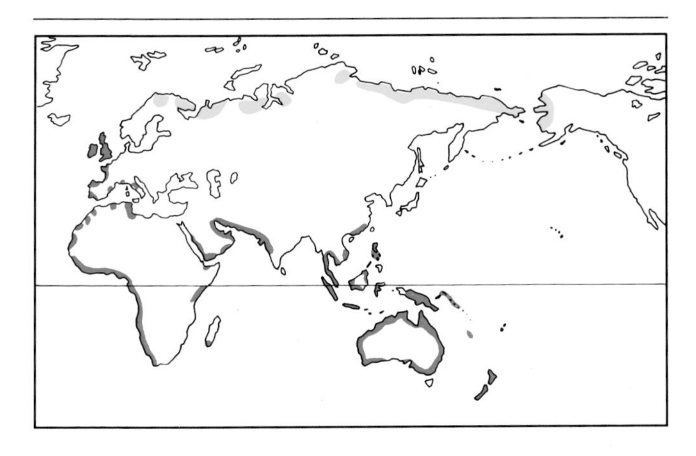

Range Northern Scandinavia eastward to the westernmost part of Alaska close to the Arctic Circle between latitudes 65° and 75° north. Winters along the shores well to the south in Africa, with a sporadic distribution to India, south-east Asia, and Australia. Concentrations of up to 600,000 birds are recorded in Mauritania, north-west Africa, while 60 percent of birds remaining in Europe are found around British coasts. The sub-species *Limosa lapponica baueri* breeds in Alaska. In winter plumage it might be mistaken for a Marbled Godwit and appears sparingly along the American Pacific coast. The European bird is a rare visitor to the Atlantic coast, with only a handful of records.

RECORD OF SIGHTINGS	
Date ______	Date ______
Place ______	Place ______
Male(s) ______ Female(s) ______	Male(s) ______ Female(s) ______
Immature ______ Eclipse ______	Immature ______ Eclipse ______
Behavior Notes	

In winter plumage

Greenshank

Tringa nebularia 12–13½ in

Identification In summer the dull gray upperparts are spotted, streaked and blotched with black and brown, with head and neck finely streaked. The underparts are white. The longish bill is slightly upturned, while the long legs are greenish, giving the bird its name. In winter looks much paler, but at all times the extensive white V up the back, along with the dark wings and the call, help to identify this bird. Though often probes and picks for food, quite frequently sieves the ooze or chases small fish through the shallows. When alarmed it will bob like the Redshank. On its breeding grounds it will perch freely on stone walls, fences or rocks, from where it will often sing.
Voice A triple fluty "tchu, tchu, tchu."
Habitat Nests in swamps and marshes, clearings in the taiga, bogs, and on the tundra. At other times is found on marshes, along rivers, borders of lakes and reservoirs, salt marshes, and estuaries. Less frequently noted on the seashore.
Food Crustaceans, molluscs, and other marine invertebrates, also small fish and amphibians.

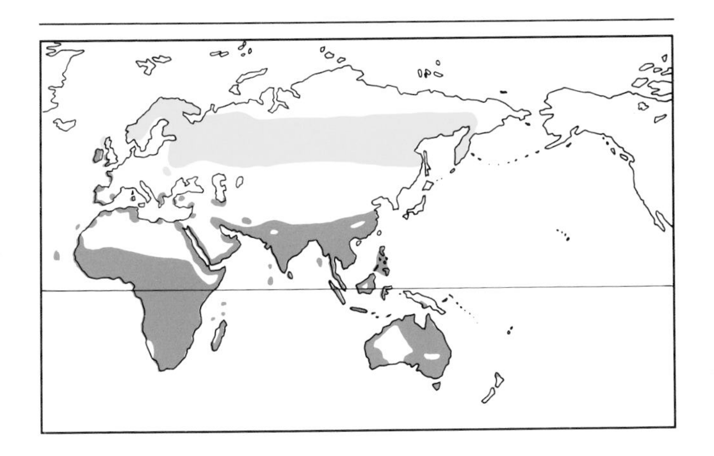

Range Breeds in Scotland eastward across northern Europe through Asia to the Kamchatka Peninsula. In spring birds return to their nesting grounds throughout May and June.
Movements In fall they are on the move by early August, when Scandinavian birds and those that breed in the USSR migrate south to winter beyond the Sahara. Up to 2000 individuals winter in Britain and Ireland, most of which are to be found in south-west Ireland. American birdwatchers are not too familiar with this species, for it has only occurred with any regularity in the Aleutians and Pribilovs. There are alleged sightings on the Atlantic seaboard, and reports of birds that have wandered south to Argentina and Chile.

RECORD OF SIGHTINGS	
Date ______	Date ______
Place ______	Place ______
Male(s) ____ Female(s) ____	Male(s) ____ Female(s) ____
Immature ____ Eclipse ____	Immature ____ Eclipse ____
Behavior Notes	

Spotted Redshank

Tringa erythropus 11½–13 in

Identification In winter plumage may be mistaken for Redshank but has a larger, more slender neck and long, attenuated rear-end, as opposed to the more dumpy, rounded redshank. The upperparts are much clearer in appearance, formed by a light gray base interspersed by uniformly white-edged feathers. A thick, black stripe through the eye emphasizes a very white eyebrow. The underparts are whiter, with finer streaking. The bill and legs are much longer, the latter usually being dark red. In flight there is a white rump with no white in wings. In breeding dress unmistakable, with all sooty-black plumage evenly sprinkled with small, bright white spots over its back and wings, this "peppered" look giving rise to the name.
Habitat Nests in open marshy areas but also favors dry areas among forest marshes. In winter mostly found on coastal and freshwater lagoons. On migration occurs at inland locations around the edges of reservoirs and pools.

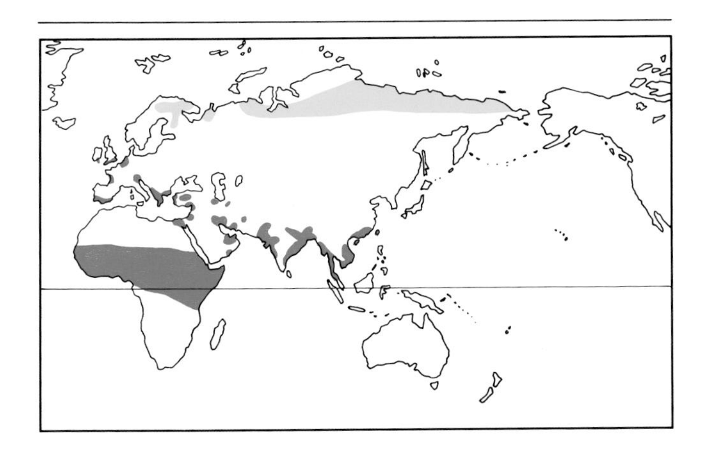

Food Worms, crustaceans, and insect larvae, plus water beetles, newts, and small frogs; on breeding grounds frantically chases and snatches newly-hatched mosquitos.
Range Breeds from northern Sweden eastward to eastern Siberia. Mainly winters in the Mediterranean region, also Africa south to the Equator and sometimes as far south as South Africa. Commoner in West Africa than East Africa. Also occurs eastward to northern Pakistan, south-east India, Sri Lanka, Burma, southern China, and Japan.
Movements There are only one or two reports of this bird reaching the North American continent.

RECORD OF SIGHTINGS	
Date ________	Date ________
Place ________	Place ________
Male(s) ____ Female(s) ____	Male(s) ____ Female(s) ____
Immature ____ Eclipse ____	Immature ____ Eclipse ____
Behavior Notes	

In winter plumage

Wood Sandpiper

Tringa glareola 7½–8 in

Identification Breeding adults have gray-brown upperparts, which are boldly speckled white, and white underparts, save for some brown streaking on the neck and breast. In winter plumage the upperparts are less clearly speckled and the breast is grayish with much finer streaking. Juveniles are warmer brown above, with buff spots and fine brown streaks on the breast, which is initially washed buff but fades to white by late fall. At all ages and seasons, the white eyebrow is prominent. Confusion is most likely with the Green Sandpiper, but is smaller, slimmer and longer legged (these are yellowish). In flight looks more slender, the legs project well beyond the tail and shows much less contrast between the dark wings and white rump than a Green Sandpiper.
Voice A characteristic "chiff-if" or chiff, iff-iff."

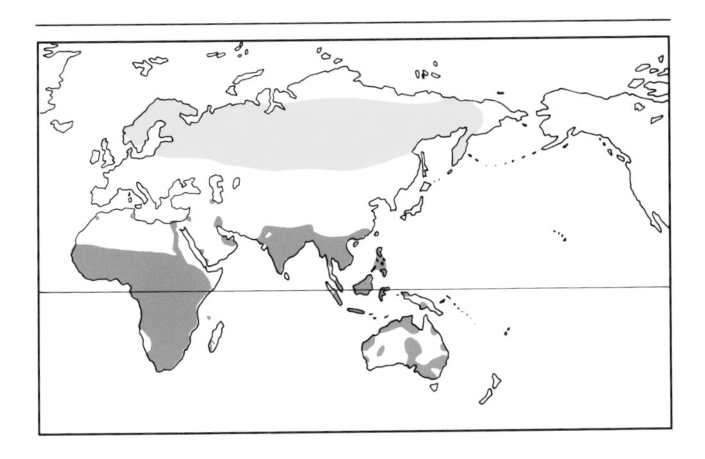

Habitat In breeding season damp conifer or birch woods, boggy moorland, or marshes are chosen. At other times marshy areas, muddy margins of freshwater lakes and pools.
Food Freshwater and terrestrial insects, particularly beetles.
Range Breeds from Scandinavia across northern Russia, and sporadically into the Aleutian Islands and Alaska. Nests sparingly in Scotland, with about half a dozen pairs at several scattered localities. Most winter in Africa, but exceptionally a few remain as far north as Britain outside the breeding season.
Movements Has occurred as a vagrant along the eastern seaboard of the USA.

RECORD OF SIGHTINGS	
Date ______	Date ______
Place ______	Place ______
Male(s) ______ Female(s) ______	Male(s) ______ Female(s) ______
Immature ______ Eclipse ______	Immature ______ Eclipse ______
Behavior Notes	

In winter plumage

Common Sandpiper

Actitus hypoleucos 7½–8 in

Identification Easily distinguished from similar small sandpipers (except Spotted Sandpiper) by the continual bobbing motion of its tail end, which is most obvious when it walks or perches on rocks or boulders. The upperparts are brown, with patches on the side of the upper breast. There is a white "peak" between the breast patch and the folded wing area, and the underparts are white. There is a shortish, straight bill and the short legs are usually a pale grayish color. The flight, usually a foot or so above the water, consists of a regular, peculiar flickering wingbeat and momentary glide on down-curved wings unique to the species. When disturbed, it often flies out over the water, returning to the shore in a wide arc, landing 300 feet or so from its starting point. There is a well-defined wing bar and white either side of the tail. The sexes are similar. In fall juveniles are quite heavily barred on the wing coverts.
Voice A far-carrying "dee-dee-dee-dee." On breeding grounds song is "kitti-wee wit, kitti-wee wit" uttered in flight or on ground.
Habitat In breeding season favors fast-running streams or borders of lakes, lochs and tarns, usually in or close to hilly country. Occasionally chooses more lowland areas. Outside breeding season found along rivers, streams, margins of reservoirs, sand and gravel workings. Also occurs along river estuaries, but rarely on open mudflats.

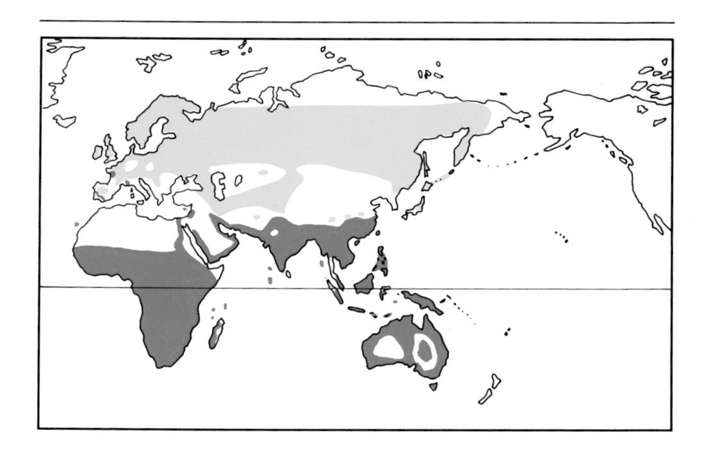

Food Insects, worms, small molluscs, and crustaceans.
Range Breeds extensively in most parts of Britain and Europe eastward through Asia to China and Japan. European birds winter south of the Sahara, while those of Asian origin move to India, south-east Asia, and some reach Australia.
Movements Some birds are on the move in March but main passage is late April or early May. Return south after nesting often as early as July. Main movement in August, but noted well into September and even October. About 100 individuals winter in the southern half of Britain every year. A rare visitor to the outer Aleutians, the Pribilov Islands, and St Lawrence Island. Vagrants have reached western Alaska.

RECORD OF SIGHTINGS	
Date ______	Date ______
Place ______	Place ______
Male(s) ______ Female(s) ______	Male(s) ______ Female(s) ______
Immature ______ Eclipse ______	Immature ______ Eclipse ______
Behavior Notes	

Curlew Sandpiper

Calidris ferruginea 7–9 in

Identification Similar in size to a Dunlin but more delicately built and elegant in behavior. Its long, decurved black bill, slender neck, and long black legs produce a characteristic outline. Breeding adults have rich chestnut heads, necks and underparts, apart from their undertail coverts, which are white. The upperparts are a mixture of black feathers with chestnut fringes and white tips on the scapulars, while the wing coverts are gray-brown with whitish fringes. Females have paler underparts with some white feathers and dark brown barring on the belly. In non-breeding plumage it is gray-brown above and white below; there is a long white supercilium. Juveniles are similar to non-breeding birds but have browner upperparts, with a scaly appearance and a buff wash to the neck and breast. The flight is swift when they show their white wing bars and distinctive white rump.

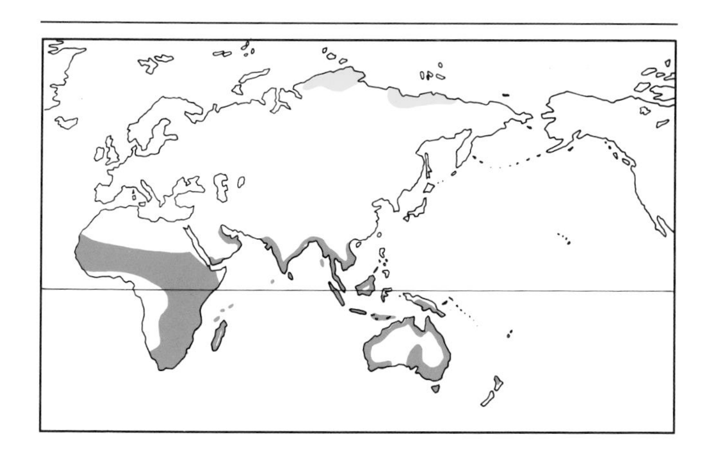

Voice A characteristic rippling "chirrup."
Habitat Favored breeding area is Arctic tundra, with abundant rich, boggy pools and hollows fed by melting snow. In winter favors both muddy and sandy shores, tidal creeks, and the muddy margins of freshwater pools.
Food Crustaceans, molluscs, insects, and some vegetable matter.
Range Occurs as a rare vagrant in North America.
Movements In spring birds follow a direct route from winter quarters in Africa across Italy and south-eastern Europe. Return passage can begin as early as late June when the first males leave. Females follow in July. Juveniles are the last to leave in August.

RECORD OF SIGHTINGS	
Date ______	Date ______
Place ______	Place ______
Male(s) ______ Female(s) ______	Male(s) ______ Female(s) ______
Immature ____ Eclipse ______	Immature ____ Eclipse ______
Behavior Notes	

In winter plumage

Little Stint

Calidris minuta 4½–5½ in

Identification Noticeably smaller than the commoner Dunlin, it has a shorter, finer black bill and black legs. Birds in breeding plumage have rufous heads, necks and breasts with brown streaks. The black back feathers have bright rufous edges which add to their smart appearance. The underparts are white, except for a buff wash and slight streaking on the upper breast. In winter adults are basically brownish-gray above and white underneath. The juvenile has a dark rufous crown accentuated by lateral white stripes and bold, white supercilium. The nape is gray, and the dark, upper feathers are fringed rufous and white with very distinctive white edges to the mantle, which forms a marked V on the back. The underparts are again white, except for a buff breast, which is streaked at the sides. In flight there is a clear white wing bar and white sides on the rump and tail.

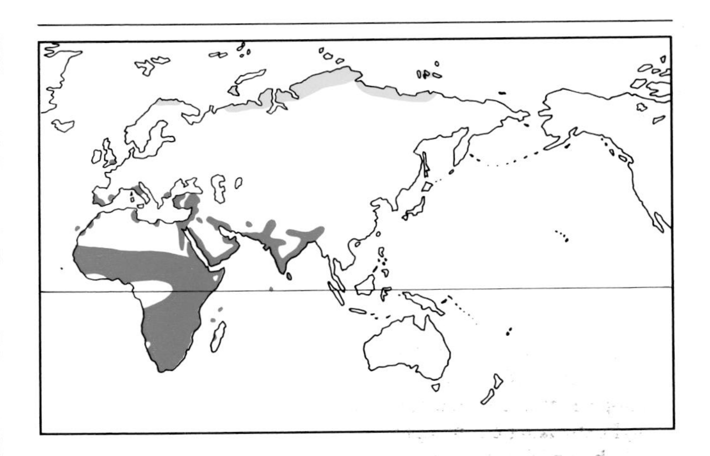

Voice Usual call is a short, low-pitched "tit" or "chit."
Habitat Breeds in the Arctic tundra. At other times mainly coastal, though some do occur inland.
Food Invertebrates, such as insects, beetles, worms and small molluscs, and crustaceans.
Range Nests in Scandinavia and northern Russia. Most winter in Africa around the Mediterranean, or in India.
Movements Moves northwards to breeding grounds between April and early June. After nesting, adults return southward followed in late August by juveniles. Passage often continues into October. A few overwinter. Very rarely turns up in the USA.

RECORD OF SIGHTINGS	
Date ________	Date ________
Place ________	Place ________
Male(s) ____ Female(s) ____	Male(s) ____ Female(s) ____
Immature ____ Eclipse ____	Immature ____ Eclipse ____
Behavior Notes	

A juvenile in autumn

Temminck's Stint

Calidris temminckii 5–6 in

Identification A tiny, mouse-like wader, distinguished from other small sandpipers and stints by its plain, dull appearance. In breeding plumage the mantle and scapular feathers have black centers and buff edges, which give it a darker, drabber appearance than the Little Stint, while the head and breast is mottled and streaked brown on a gray background. The chin and belly are white, and there is an indistinct pale supercilium. Non-breeding birds are more unifom. In flight shows a short, narrow, white wing bar, also white sides to rump and distinctive white outer tail feathers; most obvious on take-off and landing.
Voice A quick, dry "tirrirrirri" rattle, usually uttered when flushed, at which time frequently "towers," like Common Snipe.
Habitat Tundra with short turfy areas, or sandy, gravelly shorelines of freshwater pools and islets, also sheltered valleys with plenty of mossy bogs, damp grassland, and dwarf willow scrub for

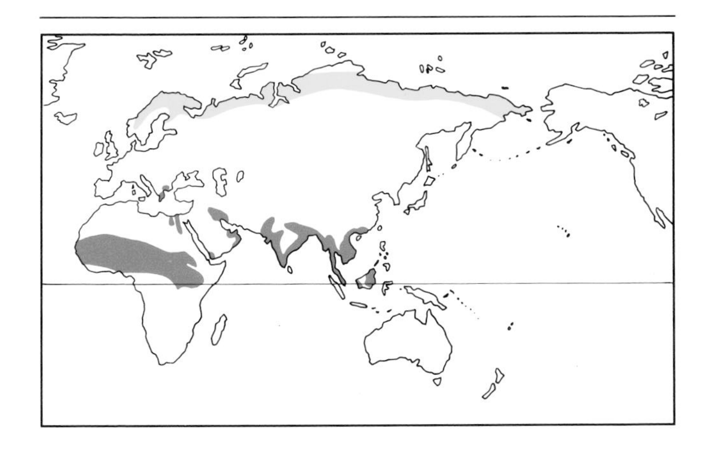

nesting. At other times sheltered muddy backwaters and salt-marshes, inland waters, irrigated areas, but rarely on coast.
Food Insects and their larvae, especially beetles and flies.
Range In the USA the species has been recorded as a vagrant in both spring and fall on the Aleutian Islands and in western Alaska, St Lawrence Islands, the Pribilov Islands and Vancouver, British Columbia.
Movements Birds return northwards and pass through Europe between mid-April and mid-May. Southward passage is quite leisurely, beginning when adults leave in July and continuing until the juveniles reach their wintering grounds in October.

RECORD OF SIGHTINGS	
Date ______	Date ______
Place ______	Place ______
Male(s) ______ Female(s) ______	Male(s) ______ Female(s) ______
Immature ______ Eclipse ______	Immature ______ Eclipse ______
Behavior Notes	

In winter plumage

Ruff

Philomachus pugnax 10–13 in (male)
8–9½ in (female)

Identification A medium-to-large bird with a small head, long neck, medium-length, slightly decurved bill and long legs. The males are much larger than females. During the breeding season the male is particularly distinctive with an Elizabethan-style ruff and ear tufts whose colors vary from individual to individual, from white through buff and rust to black, either barred or plain. The bill and legs are yellow to red. Females in breeding plumage are also variable in appearance but have a dark brown head, breast and upperparts, with many dark feather centers and dark spotting on the breast and flanks. Juveniles have neatly scaled upperparts with blackish center feathers, especially in the scapulars fringed buff to white. The bill is black and legs blackish. In flight all Ruffs show prominent white ovals at the sides of the rump and a white wing bar.
Voice Generally silent, but very occasionally utters a quiet "tu-whit."
Habitat In breeding season is found in low-lying tundra with lakes and marshes, to damp grasslands and meadow in the more southern parts of its range. On passage and in winter favors grassland, freshwater margins, paddies, and coastal lagoons. Rarely on coast.

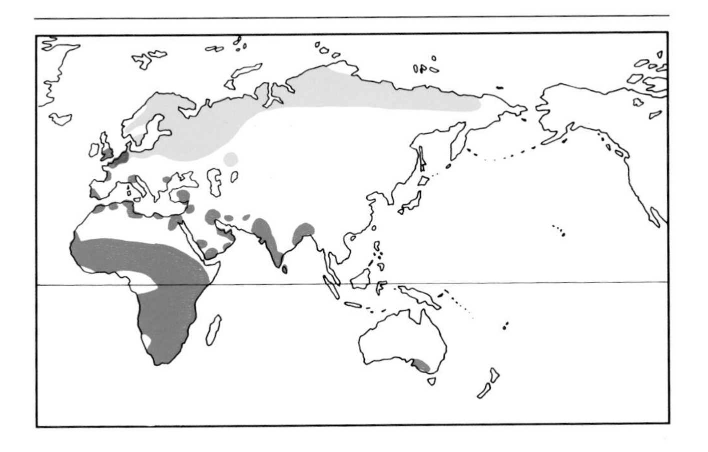

Food Chiefly insects, also worms, small freshwater molluscs, small crustaceans, also vegetable matter at times.
Range Breeds across northern Europe and Asia from the British Isles to eastern Siberia. Virtually the entire Ruff population winters in Africa, mostly in a strip from Senegal and Gambia to Sudan. A vagrant to Bermuda, Madagascar, and South America, regularly occurring in the USA and Canada, where it is noted on both coasts and in the interior. Nested in Alaska in 1976.
Movements A common migrant throughout Europe, northward passage starts in February and lasts until May. Autumn movement begins with the usual protracted passage of males from early July, followed by females and juveniles lasting until October.

RECORD OF SIGHTINGS	
Date ______	Date ______
Place ______	Place ______
Male(s) ____ Female(s) ____	Male(s) ____ Female(s) ____
Immature ____ Eclipse ____	Immature ____ Eclipse ____
Behavior Notes	

In winter plumage

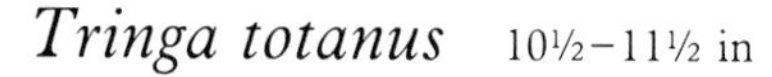

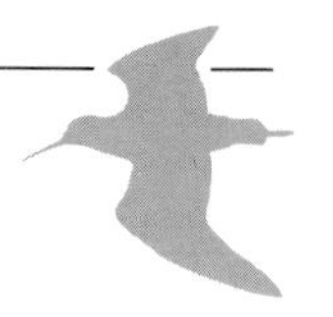

Redshank

Tringa totanus 10½–11½ in

Identification A noisy, usually unapproachable bird, flying up at the first hint of danger, revealing conspicuous white rear edges to the dark wings and white back and rump, giving a very black and white appearance. On landing, it noticeably holds wings raised above its back for a moment or so, showing a very white underwing. In summer the rich brown upperparts, head and neck are strongly streaked and speckled. In winter loses its warm brown coloring and looks quite gray. At all times the long, reddish bill tipped with black, and the vermilion red legs are distinctive. The legs of young birds are quite yellowish, as are adults in winter. **Voice:** A musical "tuhu" and triple "tu-hu-hu." Also has a single alarm note "teuk."
Habitat In breeding season equally at home on sand dunes, saltings, and coastal marshes, while inland favors marshes, grassy waterside meadows, margins of lakes and reservoirs, and the like. In winter mudflats and tidal estuaries are mostly frequented.
Food Molluscs, crustaceans, and worms. At inland locations earthworms, cranefly larvae, vegetable matter, seeds and berries are also taken.

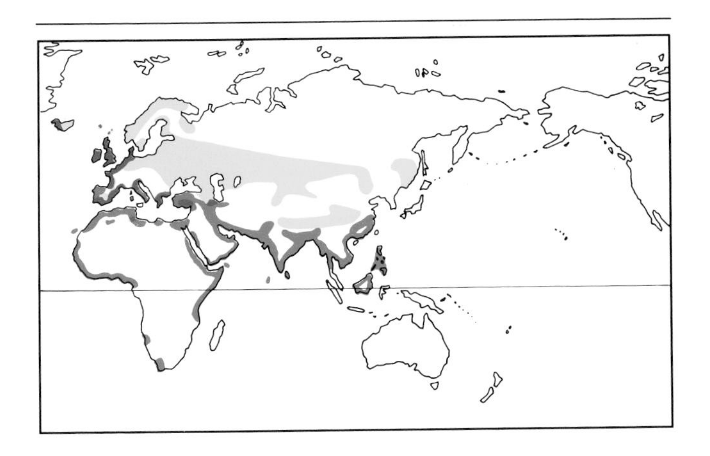

Range Breeds in Iceland, Britain and Ireland, Scandinavia and scattered inland areas of Eastern Europe and eastward across Russia. Winters around coasts of Britain and Europe, also Mediterranean region and south to West Africa.
Movements Birds return to their breeding grounds as early as January or February, though more typically March. In more northern climes it can be May before they arrive. By July nesting has been completed and birds begin their drift back to the coast and south to other wintering zones. There are only one or two reports of this bird reaching the North American continent.

RECORD OF SIGHTINGS	
Date ______	Date ______
Place ______	Place ______
Male(s) ______ Female(s) ______	Male(s) ______ Female(s) ______
Immature ______ Eclipse ______	Immature ______ Eclipse ______
Behavior Notes	

Green Sandpiper

Tringa ochropus 8–9½ in

Identification At a distance this medium-small, stocky bird looks dark above and white below, but close views reveal a white eye-ring, a distinct white supercilium in front of the eye, and fine olive-brown streaks on the chin and throat. These become denser on the breast and flanks, where they merge into blotches. The legs and bill are dark. In breeding plumage the upperparts have whitish spots, but by August have mostly gone. Juveniles are paler and browner-looking. Very distinctive in flight with dark back and wings, and a startlingly white rump, looking like a large House Martin.
Voice A loud ringing "klu-weet-weeta-weeta" and a rippling "tu-loo-ee."
Habitat Forest swamps in breeding season; at other times a variety of shallow, inland freshwater sites, with a marked aversion for coastal or tidal habitats.
Food A variety of aquatic invertebrates, and sometimes small fish.
Range Breeds in Scandinavia and eastern Europe through to Siberia. Has bred in Britain. Main wintering areas are in Central Africa, the Mediterranean basin and from Turkey and Iran eastward through India to China. However, some winter in more temperate parts of western Europe, including Britain, where up to

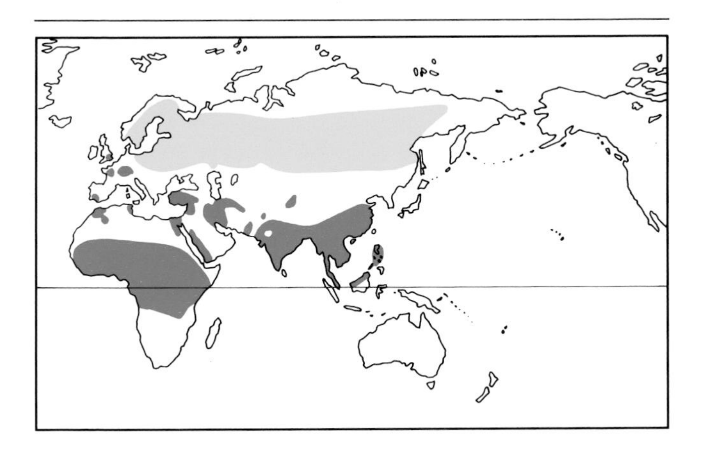

1000 birds may be present mainly scattered throughout south-east England.

Movements The northwards movement through Europe peaks in late April and May, though some birds are still passing through in May. Migration occurs on a broad front, but numbers are small and passage is swift. Females disperse early from the nesting grounds and this species is one of the first migrants to head south again. By the end of June, birds are noted moving through Britain. Most occur in August, when small gatherings can be seem at favored sites. Concentrations of more than 50 are quite exceptional. A vagrant to the outer Aleutian Islands.

RECORD OF SIGHTINGS	
Date ______	Date ______
Place ______	Place ______
Male(s) ______ Female(s) ______	Male(s) ______ Female(s) ______
Immature ______ Eclipse ______	Immature ______ Eclipse ______
Behavior Notes	

Eskimo Curlew

Numenius borealis 11½–13½ in

Identification At three-quarters of the size of a Whimbrel, this tiny curlew is much smaller than any other American curlew. However, care over its identification is necessary as, like the North American race of Whimbrel it also has a dark rump. Its striped head is also similar, though the pattern is less well-defined. An important distinction is the cinnamon tone to the underparts and underwing. In addition, its inner primaries are plain rather than notched, and barred with off-white.
Voice A rippling "tr-tr-tr" (the Inuit name was an onomatopeic pi-i-pi-uk) and a whistled "bee-bee."
Habitat/Range/Movements Formerly abundant, it was shot virtually to extinction between 1850 and 1890. In recent years a few have been observed on migration, most regularly on the coast of Texas at Galveston Island. In addition, two specimens were seen in possible breeding habitat to the west of Hudson Bay in 1976.

Winters on the pampas of South America from southern Brazil to central Argentina.

Little is known of the breeding biology of the species beyond the fact that the clutch of four, occasionally three, eggs is laid in the second half of June. All the eggs now held in museums were collected by one man, Roderick MacFarland, between the Mackenzie and Coppermine rivers. Though there are no records, the fledging period is probably very short, with birds leaving for their winter quarters immediately after fledging.

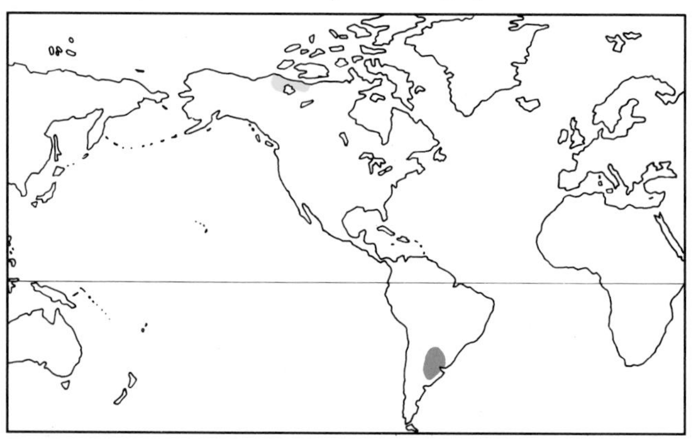

Appendix

The following is a list of species not included in the main text, but which have been recorded either very rarely or intermittently in North America.

Double-striped Thick-knee

Burhinus bistriatus

OTHER NAMES Double-striped Stone-curlew, Mexican Thick-knee
Breeds in northern South America and parts of Central America. Usually sedentary but odd individuals have reached Curaçao and Texas, where one was shot in 1961.

Lesser Sand Plover

Charadrius mongolus

OTHER NAMES Mongolian Plover, Mongolian Sand Plover, Mongolian Dotterel
Breeds in scattered localities from eastern Asia to north-east Siberia and rarely Alaska; winters on coasts from East Africa to Australia. Strongly migratory, with vagrants to Spain, Norway, Poland, Austria, eastern Mediterranean, parts of Africa, west Alaska, Yukon Territory, Ontario, Oregon, California, and Louisiana.

Red-necked Stint

Calidris ruficollis

OTHER NAMES Rufous-necked Stint, Rufous-necked Sandpiper
Breeds in north and north-east Siberia and occasionally west Alaska; winters in south-east Asia and Australasia. In North America a vagrant to south-east Alaska, British Columbia, Oregon, California, the Atlantic coast of the USA, and Bermuda.

Long-toed Stint

Calidris subminuta

Breeds in Siberia; winters in south-east Asia, the Philippines and Australasia. A vagrant to Sweden, British Isles (one record), west Aleutians, western Alaska, and Oregon, plus one or two places in East Africa and the Indian Ocean.

Sharp-tailed Sandpiper

Calidris acuminata

OTHER NAME Siberian Pectoral Sandpiper
Breeds in northern Siberia; winters in Australasia. Regular passage migrant to western Alaska. A vagrant to Canada and the USA (mostly on Pacific coast), Scandinavia, France, the British Isles (19 records), and parts of Asia.

Cox's Sandpiper

Calidris paramelantos

First described in 1982 on basis of specimens collected in South Australia. Breeding area unknown, but probably somewhere in USSR. A juvenile caught, ringed and photographed at Duxbury Beach, Massachusetts, USA, 15 September 1987. This is only the second record of the "species" away from the Australian wintering grounds, the other reported in Hong Kong, spring 1987.

Spoon-billed Sandpiper

Eurynorhynchus pygmeus

OTHER NAME Spoonbill Sandpiper
A rare breeder in eastern Siberia; winters in south-east Asia. A vagrant to west Aleutians, west Alaska, and Vancouver.

Great Snipe

Gallinago media

OTHER NAME Double Snipe
Breeds in the mountains of Scandinavia and from eastern Poland to the river Yenisei in Siberia. One record in USA – New Jersey, September 1963.

Woodcock

Scolopax rusticole

OTHER NAME Eurasian Woodcock
Breeds across the temperate forest zone of Eurasia. Has been recorded in Newfoundland and Quebec, south to Alabama, and even inland in Ohio.

Little Whimbrel

Numenius minutus

OTHER NAME Little Curlew
Rare breeder in central and north-east Siberia; winters in Australasia. Vagrant to British Isles (two records), Norway, California, and a few other scattered areas outside Europe and North America.

Bristle-thighed Curlew

Numenius tahitiensis

A rare wader that breeds in west Alaska; winters on Pacific islands. A vagrant to a number of west Pacific localities and in North America to south Alaska, Vancouver Island, British Columbia, and Washington.

Slender-billed Curlew

Numenius tenuirostris

A very rare breeder from central Siberia; winters in the Mediterranean basin. Records are very few. Vagrants have occurred in Oman, the Canaries and Azores, Netherlands, Germany, Poland, and the Canadian shore of Lake Erie, where one was collected in about 1925.

Curlew

Numenius arquata

OTHER NAMES Eurasian Curlew, European Curlew, Common Curlew
Breeds from Britain eastward to Siberia, and from Scandinavia and Russia in the north to France, through to the Balkans and beyond to the Kirghez Steppes. A vagrant to Massachusetts, New York, Jan Mayer and Bear Island.

Index

Acknowledgments

I am grateful to the many photographers for the excellence of their illustrations. Their names are listed here against the page number where their photographs appear.

Front cover top: R.T. Mills bottom: D.K. Richards

2–3 Colin Smith
6–7 A.J. Bond
8–9 S.C. Brown
10 M.C. Wilkes
11 R.T. Mills
12–13 M.C. Wilkes
14 J.B. & S. Bottomley
16 H. Cruikshank/Vireo
18 E. Soothill
20 J. Lawton Roberts
22 J. Lawton Roberts
24 E. Soothill
26 M.C. Wilkes
28 T. Leach
30 W. Lankinen
32 Hanne & Jens Eriksen
34 R. Glover
36 Tom Leach
38 R.P. Tipper
40 M.C. Wilkes
42 W. Lankinen
44 S. & B.A. Craig
46 W. Lankinen
48 M.C. Wilkes
50 M.C. Wilkes
52 W. Lankinen
54 Gordon Langsbury
56 W. Lankinen
58 A. Morris/Vireo
60 J.B. & S. Bottomley
62 R. Glover
64 S.P. Myers/Vireo
66 M.C. Wilkes
68 J.B. & S. Bottomley
70 W. Lankinen
72 M.C. Wilkes
74 W. Lankinen
76 W. Lankinen
78 R.J. Chandler
80 Hanne & Jens Eriksen
82 P.C. Conners/Vireo
84 H.A. Hems
86 R. Glover
88 M.C. Wilkes
90 Hanne & Jens Eriksen
92 W. Lankinen
94 Dr J. Davies
96 M.C. Wilkes
98 D.M. Cotteridge
100 R.T. Mills
102 R.T. Mills
104 G.R. Jones

106 J.B. & S. Bottomley
108–9 R. Glover
110 R. Maier
112 M.C. Wilkes
114 R.T. Mills
116 R. Glover
118 C. Greaves
120 Hanne & Jens Eriksen
122 M.C. Wilkes
124 M.C. Wilkes
126 C. Greaves
128 P. Doherty
130 C. Greaves
132 M.C. Wilkes
134 M.C. Wilkes
136 A.T. Moffet

Title Page Waders flock over the Dee Estuary

The American Birding Association, Inc. (ABA) is pleased to endorse these illustrated pocket guide books about North American birds. The Association is a membership organization which exists to promote the recreational observation and study of wild birds, to educate the public in the appreciation of birds and their contribution to the environment, to assist the study of birds in their natural habitats, and to contribute to the development of improved methods of bird population studies. All persons interested in these aspects of bird study are invited to join.

All members receive *Birding*, the official publication of the Association, and its monthly newsletter *Winging It*. Members are served by ABA Sales which offers a wide spectrum of publications related to identification and geographical distribution of birds. ABA sponsors bird-related tours of various lengths to a variety of localities both in the United States and abroad. Finally, the Association holds biennial conventions of its members in the United States or Canada which feature field trips and identification workshops.

Any person wishing information about membership or any related services is invited to contact the Association at:

American Birding Association Inc.
P.O. Box 6599
Colorado Springs, CO 80934
Telephone: (800) 634-7736